# THE
# PENNY PINCHER'S BOOK
# REVISITED

*Living Better for Less*

## JOHN AND IRMA MUSTOE

SOUVENIR PRESS

First published in 2007 by Souvenir Press Ltd,
43 Great Russell Street, London WC1B 3PD

Portions of this book appeared in slightly different form in
*The Penny Pincher's Book* (Souvenir Press).

ISBN 9780285637979

Typeset by M Rules

Printed and bound in Great Britain

# CONTENTS

# INTRODUCTION

In this book you will find hundreds of ways of living better for less. Some of the ideas can save you hundreds of pounds a year, others just a few pounds. Some ideas are rather fun, others a bit laborious for the savings made. The whole book can be read on this level, and you can choose out of it ideas that are relevant to your life.

Underneath what we hope are a lot of good ideas there is another big idea: how to make life more satisfying.

The Penny Pincher's Book Revisited comes out of our life experience and out of six years publishing *The Penny Pincher Paper*. There are just so many good ideas on how to save money, and not one of them is revolutionary. Economy diets of oatmeal and peanut butter do not make it into this book. You will find no mention of how to weave your own clothes. Nor is there within this book advice on investments or going in for competitions.

If you are looking for ways to be mean and grasping, put this book down now.

It is about living better, not piling up riches. It is based on the premise that if we look after our money with the same diligence that we apply to earning it, then we will live better, more fulfilling lives. One way to overcome money worries is to earn more. If you can. If earning more is unlikely, as it is for most people, then spending better is the answer.

We have always said that 'penny-pinching' (and there *must* be a better word for it) is part of a way of life which includes concern for the world around us, pride in things that we make and mend and a desire to keep traditions which were handed down to us. What it is not, though – we have always tried to show that it is not – is being miserly, niggardly, mean and single-mindedly pinching every penny whether that penny needs pinching or not, just for the sake of penny-pinching. The word for that is downright stinginess.

In our married life together we have had long periods when we were making good money, working hard, and having a miserable time. We could not afford the holiday for the children that would have meant so much to them. We were sick with worry over the mortgage payments. Our bank would write us letters beginning 'We thought you would like to know that your overdraft has reached …' when of course we did not want to know anything of the kind.

In other years our joint income was very low. Some years our little company ran at a loss. Those were not good times either, but they were not significantly worse than when we were earning big money.

We looked around us, and our experience seemed to be common. Some low-income people are happy and some high-income people are in despair. Some people on low incomes are sunk in misery and some wealthy people are full of joy.

Maybe, we thought, it is not how much money we earn that is

crucial, but how much we spend relative to the amount we earn. Mr. Micawber, Dickens' character in *David Copperfield*, was not the first or last to find that if expenditure exceeds income, even by a little, then misery is the result. That's when we started publishing *The Penny Pincher Paper*: the response has been overwhelming.

The first thing that penny pinchers try to achieve is to cut down slightly on their expenditure, so that income covers outgoings. Now money is not a black cloud over our heads, but is just one of those things that we use to give quality to our lives.

Money is treated as an essential, but not ruling, factor. A dozen small economies and a lot of planning give control. Now money can be spent to give us greater satisfaction.

Spending money must be a skill at least as important as earning it. Making things last has got to be equal to buying something new. There is more satisfaction to be had from making your own than in making do with something produced in a factory. We like to think that our ideas in this book will trigger in you new ideas that will make sense to you in your journey through life.

On the subject of our journey through life, it is not unreasonable that future generations should ask this generation, you and me, to leave the world in at least as good condition as we found it. Let us be bold and try to leave it in a little better shape if we can.

This book will not solve all the World's environmental problems, but all the ideas here will help. Every idea you come up with to get control of your money will also lessen your demands on the resources of the World.

Read on. Learn to make and to mend, and to cut out waste so you can focus on what you do want. With the money saved there are choices before you. If you can then afford it, buy a cottage in Normandy, learn Italian, take the children camping in Scotland, start an environmental group, or even put the stuff into savings. They are all good choices. They are all choices for you to make.

Have fun with your money!

# 1

## Let's Make a Start on Living Better for Less

To some people a restricted income doesn't matter a bit, in fact it often seems to help as a means for getting a lot of reality out of life ... Lack of initiative is the thing that really cripples one.

SAKI

We have always been interested in making things ourselves, whether clothes, food, furniture, or 'artsy-craftsy' things such as candles, rugs, and spare parts for machinery when we had to.

The more we made these things, the more we realised that we were saving a great deal of money by not buying in more than we needed, and sometimes our bank manager agreed that this was a smart move.

We had also, from the very earliest days of our marriage, taken a decision to use as few chemicals and poisons as possible and this includes insecticides, herbicides, drugs from aspirin to tranquilisers, and miracle potions.

There you have the triangle – self-reliance, thrift, environmental friendliness. Call them what you will, the three aspects are interdependent, and no matter which one catches your interest first, the other two will develop to some degree.

It would be unusual to find someone who cares about the earth's environment but wastes money and knows nothing about making things for themselves, just as people who tend towards arts and crafts can always find artistic supplies in everyday things around them such as leaves, bark, metal, scraps of fabric. The thrifty are very quickly self-reliant – often almost self-sufficient – and being environmentally friendly is just second nature to them.

We believe that these strengths contribute to a sustainable lifestyle, not just for ourselves but to the community and to the world in general. Not everyone will involve themselves equally in each of the three aspects, but we have noticed over the years that the three do tend to move towards each other, and anything you do in any of these areas contributes to the other two.

One of the most popular articles in our *Penny Pincher Paper* was the 30-Uses series, where we listed 31 ways to recycle things that were about to be discarded. This was not a how-to guide, but examples of how to look anew at an item, to 'see things that weren't there', to use what one already had. Here are 30 uses for old shoes:

1. Cut leather washers from leather shoes.
2. Use old shoe laces, especially long ones, for sewing onto tool kit made from old blue jeans.
3. Shoe tongues can be fastened into the bracket for a door handle on a Morris Minor.

4. Entire sole, especially of trainers/tennis shoes, etc., makes WONDERFUL hinge for duck house door.
5. Soft tongue makes desk top for doll house – 'gold tooling' is done with gold ballpoint.
6. Canvas shoes repair canvas bags, rugs, etc.
7. Fancy shoes go straight into the dress-up box, often to be retrieved eleven years later when they return to fashion.
8. Cut circles (or squares etc), fasten/glue onto doors where they bump walls or furniture.
9. Soft slip-on shoes can be taken apart to use as patterns for more soft shoes or slippers.
10. Old shoes only in the garden!
11. Leaking Wellies become patching material to glue onto paddling pools, ground sheets, non-slip pads for underneath corners of rugs.
12. We used outgrown roller skates to move a heavy Welsh dresser [and a skateboard is ideal for moving a freezer, too].
13. Sherlock Holmes kept his pipes in an old slipper hung on the wall.
14. Two tongues can be stitched together to make a pouch/bag.
15. Use to cut out long-lasting stencil patterns.
16. Make arm and finger protectors for archery practice.
17. Cut out badges for children, attach a large safety pin with strong thread, decorate.
18. Use a strip of shoe leather to protect surfaces of furniture when using a stretcher.
19. Make a hair ornament to hold ponytails, etc., using a wooden skewer to hold hair in place. The ornament can be tooled, the skewer carved.

20. Make bookmarks with strips of leather.
21. Make a pump seal for a bicycle pump.
22. Make padding to use underneath lamps or ornaments.
23. Make small drinks coasters.
24. Make a palm pad for pushing needles into upholstery fabrics – or when sewing leather to repair other old shoes.
25. Repair leather car seats: patch inside hole, sew, dye to match if necessary.
26. Use over vice jaws to avoid marking fine-finish surfaces, and when repairing furniture.
27. Stop a rattling door or window with a piece of leather tacked to frame.
28. Small strips of leather along the broom head will protect walls and furniture.
29. Old tennis shoes can be used as kneeling mats for gardening, etc.
30. You can, if you wish, have old shoes bronzed – use as a door stop, or ornament.
31. Tie onto rear bumper of newlyweds' car, along with tin cans, etc.

Let's start, then, with the easy things that can be done to live not just for less, but *better* for less. Self-reliance means just that, depending on yourself, making and mending or recycling things before going out and buying an answer to a problem or need – or want.

'Waste not, want not' is an environmentally-friendly way to live.

There is a fine line between keeping things that will be useful and hoarding.

Buy less. Use less. Waste less.

Borrow – and return on time – a book from the library. Libraries are still free so long as you don't incur fines for over-due books.

Whether you want it or not, you have paid for the public library service through your taxes, so you might as well get some use out of it. The more you use it the lower the cost per pound of tax paid. Libraries are an opportunity to sample authors when you are uncertain whether you want to invest in a book written by them. Libraries have time-tables for trains and buses. Libraries are full of books on every craft and skill the DIY enthusiast can need. Use them.

Just as the only policeman that counts is the one inside us, the only penny pincher that makes a difference is the one you learn to be yourself.

You know you are winning when the children ask you what you want for your birthday, and you can honestly say that there is nothing you want. Of course you could think up things for them to buy, but you would not feel any better if they got them for you.

Don't waste your hard-earned money by not complaining if you have purchased something which is unsatisfactory.

If you're complaining about a service or product, do it in writing and KEEP A COPY, because phoning is expensive and companies are very adept at transferring you from one department to another.

One of the biggest money-savers there is: take care of what you have. Maintenance works.

There are many four-letter words in English but 'housewife' is not one of them.

Cut Brillo pads, nylon scourers, dusters, sponges and so on in half before using them – they go twice as far that way.

Old T-shirts make super cleaning cloths.

## Cosset your carpets

Learn to remove stains and spots from your carpets – they are among the most expensive things in your house. Be sure that they are stain-resistant when you buy them, and then never,

never, never let anything like washing-up liquid touch them! Detergents leave a sticky residue, which attracts more dirt and quite likely changes the colour of the carpet where they have been used. One roll of paper towels was a cheap price to pay for completely removing a glass of port from a white carpet. If for no other reason than that, do not eschew paper towels – just don't use them for every drop of water you spill.

Vacuuming a carpet gets the dirt out of it. This dirt will, as the carpet is walked on, cut the carpet fibres. Clean carpets make money sense.

Take off outdoor shoes when you get home – makes the shoes last longer and prevents even more dirt being deposited on your carpets.

Floors do not have to have wall-to-wall carpets. A sanded and sealed wooden floor can look very nice, and is a lot cheaper – if it was already there in the first place.

---

Most of the paintings on our walls have been done by us. They may not be good, but it is the only way we could afford original art.

There is nothing on television tonight that is worth watching, there was nothing last night, and there won't be anything tomorrow, so you might as well spend the evening working on the house.

Most of the best money spent on your house will probably not be visible. Learn how to spend wisely on your biggest investment – it isn't dried flowers or pretty curtains that protect the brickwork, but a coat of sealer that doesn't show.

## Never mind the cornflakes – just look at the packaging!

If you have inadvertently bought packaged cereals, make sure you get your money's worth by using the packaging, which is MUCH more valuable. Did you know that in scientific tests, rats that were fed the cereals were poorly nourished; those that were fed the packaging alone fared better. Surely you can learn from a rat?

Cereal boxes can be used as file-holders. You can cut off the top, trim the sides down at an angle, or use them turned sideways to hold files.

The bags inside cereal boxes are excellent for storing breads, and for using in the freezer. Wash them and use them again. And again unless used for poultry products.

Wash cereal bags and other food bags – but don't use so much washing-up liquid that it would be cheaper to buy another bag! A couple of drops suffice.

––––––––––

Instant coffee jars make excellent storage jars. You can decorate them if you feel so compelled.

Clear out those unwanted photographs – but use them as post-cards instead of throwing them away.

Old cutlery trays organise spools of thread, zips, buttons, sewing tools – and ice cube trays keep earrings and other similar fiddly little things in tidy groups.

Put empty scent bottles or talcum boxes into drawers to extend their useful life.

Special paper for lining drawers is a luxury, not a necessity. Use leftover wallpaper or go and buy a roll of 'lining paper' meant for walls.

Old tights or stockings can be used as nylon scourers. They can also be slipped securely over the vacuum cleaner tube to retrieve objects without sucking them into the cleaner.

Cut off any good fingers from rubber gloves you're discarding and use as fingershields – and you can chop the rest of the gloves into rubber bands, too – they really are good.

Surely everybody relegates their old toothbrush to the cleaning box or shoe polishing kit … don't they?

One of the prettiest packages under the Christmas tree is the one wrapped in a calendar page.

Pets will usually choose a comfortable old cardboard box with a blanket or discarded sweater of yours instead of an expensive wicker basket designer pet bed. Pets are smart.

## Recycling the recycled

Wrap Christmas ornaments in newspaper and store in strong cardboard boxes. Small delicate ones spend the year in egg boxes.

Children don't need expensive art and craft materials – they're right in front of you, with newspapers that they can draw on, tear, cut, glue, colour, find words or use to make up their own puzzles.

You won't worry so much about children making a mess of things if you underlay THEM with acres of newspaper – under the high chair, under tables while they're playing at them, near the sink while they 'help' wash up.

A large sheet of newspaper and a ridiculously large bow make a most cheerful wrap for large gifts.

Newspapers are good drawer, shelf and cupboard liners.

Shredded newspaper makes superb cat litter.

One of the cheaper games in life is 'Are you there, Moriarty?' which only requires a rolled-up newspaper and a blindfold. If you can't get a few laughs out of that, you are taking yourself much too seriously.

Newspaper is cheap packing material! Use it to protect your china and glass in a house move.

---

Plant lettuce seeds! A packet of seeds costs approximately the same as a single lettuce in shops. A 15g packet of seeds produces about 2,000 lettuces.

If you have boiled too much water in the kettle, pour it over your most despised weed. Makes you feel so much better about boiling too much in the first place, and it's better than chemicals!

Citrus fruit pips usually germinate into lovely small plants, and turn something that was going to be thrown away into something that lasts a very long time and gives a great deal of enjoyment for no extra money.

If you grow your own herbs such as rosemary and lavender, do use them in flower arrangements to add freshness to a room. Sage was made for roses.

Oranges stuck with cloves make traditional, long-lasting pomanders for the wardrobe.

Steam-iron (or freeze!) woolen clothes during winter to kill moth eggs. It's the larvae, not the flying moths, that do the damage. And conkers are very good 'mothballs' indeed.

At jumble sales and charity shops, you may not like the fashions, but consider the buttons, zips and trims, which would merit the price of the garment.

Clean suede with art gum or plastic erasers.

Every day you should work on something that will last longer than you do. Don't worry if your artistic talent is not that of Michelangelo – what you make this year may be imperfect, but it will be your children's and grandchildren's treasure, probably just because you made it.

Self-reliance leads to planning and taking responsibility for your own spending, cutting out waste and finding better products for less money – good, old-fashioned thrift.

Remember that when you buy something you are actually making TWO choices: you are choosing – or are obligated – to buy that something and therefore you are also choosing NOT TO BUY some other thing, i.e., you must forgo another purchase of that same value.

'Needs' expand to eat all available income.

It is a curious thing that we buy magazines concerned with fashion and with cars, full of articles and advertisements for things we cannot afford and would not enjoy if we had, illustrated in the lives of the most useless members of society. Save the price of the magazines and the corrosion of temptation by leaving the magazines on the shelf.

The Four Day Wait works. If you are about to buy something which isn't a necessity, and you have a little quiet voice somewhere whispering to you, listen to it, and wait four days before you make the purchase. It gives you time to compare prices elsewhere, or come up with an alternative, or even to decide that you don't need or want it.

Look after the pounds and confine your wild extravagances to the pennies.

## Looking at false economies

Buying small appliances to make work easier and then putting them away in cupboards.

Buying a garment on sale which has to be dry-cleaned and then throwing it into a washing machine to save a dry-cleaning bill.

Buying roll after roll of aluminium foil to cover a dish whose lid has broken. Buy a new covered dish.

Stocking up on so much food that much of it goes to waste.

Spending a pound's worth of petrol driving all over town or country to save a penny or so on an item.

Buying something so cheap that it doesn't last, nor does it do the job well.

It's CHEAPEST to buy the cheapest tool/paint/shoes, but not always in the long run, and you have to decide which is best. Take a saw, for example: do you need it just for one project? Today? A fairly good saw can be bought quite cheaply at the big DIY superstores. Or will you be using it often for years?

Can you wait a little while to buy one? This will give you time to look around for the best saw at the best price, and that may be a secondhand, craftsman's, well-maintained one, or you can look around industrial estates where workmen buy.

————————

Junk mail isn't ALL junk. If it has been printed on one side only, there is a free sheet of paper on the other side. You can use that for writing on, or you can make your own envelopes from it. You can cross through the address and prepaid bit on junk return envelopes, and paste on a label from your favourite charity – or take them apart, turn inside out, and reglue along the same edges as before. Often junk mail uses very expensive card or paper, so take advantage of the quality.

Short letters can be written on short pages. A second letter can be written on the chopped-off piece.

Write small.

Unless you have to post by first class, choose second class stamps.

If you need to send a parcel anywhere in the world there are lots of companies that will promise a super-efficient, overnight service. And charge you for it. Very few parcels have to be delivered next day. Next month is often good enough. Ask what their slow service would cost. The Post Office is as good as any.

Don't forget that it's cheaper to phone friends and relations after six o'clock and at weekends than it is during weekday hours.

Our French friend has a slip of paper taped to her telephone. It says 'Non.' No to salesmen, no to volunteering too much time, no to gossiping for too long.

## Babies are expensive. Yes or no?

Well, yes, actually, even if you do have generous friends-and-relations who pass on clothes and so on, but if we all waited until we could afford to have a family, we probably wouldn't have one. Still, we don't have to spend on them as though there were no tomorrow – quite the opposite, because you should be teaching them from childhood that one should be thrifty. Don't let children dictate to you what you should purchase. Be gentle if you wish, but establish very early on that you do not buy ANYTHING just because 'all the other kids have it ...' You may feel like a rat at the time, but believe me, you will have your reward when they come to you as young adults and say, 'I'm so glad you brought me up as you did.'

Newborn babies don't need lots of 'newborn' sized clothes – they only fit for ten days.

Babies' clothes sized three months do not fit for three months.

They may be old-fashioned, but cloth nappies are still the best choice for economy – better for your wallet, and for babies, and ultimately for all of us, considering the waste problem and health hazards when dumped.

Maternity wear? Not necessary – about half the time the answer lies in your husband's wardrobe – track suit bottoms, T-shirts, jumpers. For work or going out, a plain shift dress, preferably black, with lots of different tops for underneath, undoing blouse buttons as you expand. Change

accessories, and as you fish it out of the wardrobe for what feels like the millionth time, smile – it's not for much longer.

———

A tip that gives a 100 per cent saving: don't buy it. Then a few days later note with pleasure how often you are glad you didn't.

Every time you go to a burger-bar think about the huge and luscious steak you could have bought with the same money from a real butcher.

Do, please, pay the local tradesmen when their money is due, for being self-employed is hard work today. We may take a rather more detached view of big national companies, however. The utility companies have various levels of agitation, from the original invoice to the Final Demand. Find out how many steps they go through, and organise to pay at the moment before cut-off. This keeps the money in your account and not theirs, and they have lots more than you do.

In every month there is one totally unexpected bill for £50. Add into your budget a line labeled 'unexpected £50 bill'.

When you have a spare moment, sit down and work out whether working part-time is actually worth it! Do you use that extra money to buy more expensive convenience foods and extra clothes that you wouldn't need if you stayed at home? Would you prefer to stay at home? Why not work from home?

The money you earn will be taxed, the money you save is all yours.

## We thought you would like to know ...

If you don't already know how to do it, learn how to balance your bank statement. It does NOT tell you how much money you have. A bank statement is just that: a statement from the bank telling you what has GONE THROUGH your account AT THE BANK so far that month. If you want to know how much money you REALLY have on the date of that statement you must do a bank balance, or 'reconciliation' to your own record. Do this the minute your statement comes in.

Banks do not exist to help people. Banks exist to help banks make money – that is their business. They are not marriage guidance counselors or crisis counselors. If a crisis looms, the Citizens' Advice Bureau IS there to help people. Use it. It's free. It's good.

Pay bills at your bank instead of posting them, if they have Giro forms included. If you pay online you don't have any transport costs.

Turn all your attention to getting rid of your bank overdraft. This is a lot easier said than done. Persevere.

———

Know what MUST be paid and what you can afford.

Rule Number One: KNOW what you can afford. Spelt K-N-O-W, not H-O-P-E.

In Victorian times it was remarked that the rich man buying ten tons of coal paid less per ton than the poor man buying a half-hundredweight. This still applies, and buying in bulk can save you money, provided the product will be used, and you have the storage room.

Keep a record of every single penny you spend for at least one month – you'll learn a lot.

Christmas isn't just for December, it's for life. It should never come as a surprise, it comes round at exactly the same time every year – plan ahead.

Plan ahead, too, on holidays, and instead of staying in luxury – or even ordinary – hotels, have a look at bed-and-breakfasts.

Yachts cannot all be owned by millionaires, so the truth has to be that other people have different spending patterns from us – patterns that mean that they save on some things to have the money for what they really want, which is a yacht.

Credit cards have their uses, but handle them with care or they will eat you alive. They are marvelous if you want to buy something over the phone or internet, like an airline ticket but never, ever use them as a way of borrowing. I have a letter in front of me, offering me a new credit card with an 'attractive interest rate of 19.9 per cent APR'. I would hate to see an unattractive interest rate! As I write inflation is at 3.4 per cent and bank interest rate is 6 per cent. Nobody can afford to borrow at 16.5 per cent above the rate of inflation. Nothing you can buy can excuse giving that sort of money to a financial institution.

There is no such thing as 0 per cent interest. When you see that advertised, it simply means that the cost of the interest is in the purchase price. If you are in a position to pay cash, then ask for this money back. The salesman will give you a lot of guff, but ask to speak to the manager, and he may well cut the price to you for cash.

Computers are used by companies to save money. If you have a computer at home, use it the same way. Use the spreadsheet to help with budgeting. Keep your bank balance on it. Store good recipes in memory, and use it so that you do not forget important dates. Draft out a letter, and only when you are satisfied with it, print. That saves paper.

## Buy less. Use less. Waste less.

Use only as much laundry detergent as you need depending on the softness of your water. Calgon water softener works. Liquid laundry detergents are friendlier to machines.

Scrape out the lingering wash powder on the box seams, rinse out the liquid wash. These are more of those activities which, although they won't save you a fortune, give a warm glow of THRIFT.

If you iron towels and underwear you are certifiable.

Just because a washing-up bowl holds a gallon of water is no reason to put a gallon of hot water in it if half that much will do.

A tea mug holds approximately ten fluid ounces. A kettle holds approximately 50 fluid ounces. Boil only as much as you need to fill the mug and cover the element.

Use a smaller washing-up bowl, and keep the water hotter by NOT stacking all the cold dishes into the bowl.

For almost-free warm water, keep a kettle on the gas pilot light.

Smoking burns money. Give it up each day.

---

Radio is cheaper than TV.

Refrigerate candles for a few hours before using and they will burn more slowly, drip less, and give you better value for your money.

Keep your cooker clean – even if only for efficiency! Don't make it work just to heat encrusted crud.

Don't assume that just because it's a 'household hint' it is a money-saving one. Rubbing ANYTHING with a cut lemon is expensive.

Rescue a dried-out loaf of bread by dipping it into water and warming in the oven WHILE SOMETHING ELSE IS BAKING. If you have to heat up the whole oven just for the sake of one stale loaf of bread it's not penny-pinching, it's experimenting.

Roll a lemon, or other citrus fruit, with your hands, back and forth on the worktop surface, before squeezing it and you will get more juice. You can also heat the lemon to get more juice, but that means paying for the heat, so warm the lemon and yourself with the exercise – it's free.

Pack a lunch instead of eating out – and for the same amount of money that you would spend on lunch, you can pack a gourmet feast.

Pour olive oil into a pepper shaker so that you sprinkle it onto pizza, salads and so on, rather than glug it.

Buy smaller-sized eggs.

Scrape every bit of butter or margarine from the wrapper. Such a lovely parsimonious feeling.

It is actually cheaper to cook double amounts of a casserole and freeze half than it is to cook one casserole and then another one later.

Water is a good extender, much used by manufacturers; you can do it, too. Add to washing-up liquid. Add to yeast extract. Add to milk. Add to juices.

Do you THROW AWAY food? Make one meal a week clear-out-the-fridge. Don't buy too much in the first place. Plan ahead.

Upturn those sauce bottles. You paid for all the contents … get all the contents out.

Keep a container in the freezer for orange and lemon bits – and they can be grated while still frozen.

Keep sliced bread in the freezer. It thaws in seconds, so take out only what you need.

Kitchen foil and polythene bags are washable – again and again until they have been used for meat products.

It is perfectly possible to cut rolls of cling film, greaseproof and foil in half. Maybe not easy, but possible.

If you are 'too busy' to do meals that require long, slow cooking (these are usually the least expensive), learn to use your timed oven or try a slow-cooker. Then you can buy cheaper cuts of meat.

Dispensers are WONDERFUL for controlling amounts of washing-up liquid, shampoo, hand creams, cleansing liquids, etc., but you don't have to push the plunger all the way down!

Toothpaste is not one of life's necessities. Brush your teeth with bicarbonate of soda, or half-soda/half-salt.

If you do use toothpaste, don't squeeze it the entire length of the toothbrush! This is a fallacy perpetuated by the toothpaste

manufacturers and advertising departments! When have you ever seen an ad with a small amount of toothpaste on the brush? Cut back by half or more.

Get out the last little bit of shampoo, roll-ons, make-up, etc. Turn bottles on end until truly empty. This simple method will get just about everything out, but then you can cut tubes open and scoop out any lingering bits lurking in corners.

Buy a 'copy perfume' at a market stall – they are quite good!

Buy make-up from the half-price basket.

Lipbrushes get out the last memory of lipstick from tubes.

Store new bars of soap in the airing cupboard to make them hard. They last longer. Soft soaps dissolve too quickly.

A hot toddy doesn't have to have alcohol in it – try lemon and honey on their own. It must be good for you!

A shower takes less water than a bath, and a lick-and-promise session at the sink takes less than a shower. Here's another statistic (why do we tend to believe statistics instead of accepting what common sense tells us has been true all along?): a shower takes approximately seven gallons of water. A bath takes approximately 22 gallons of water. The compiler of these statistics obviously was not the possessor of teenagers. Parents of teenagers know that showers take 22 gallons, baths take 83 gallons.

Shaving up bitty pieces of soap to make a new bar will never make you rich, but it will make you a little less poor. If you make enough little savings, one day you may not be poor.

As you become a practiced penny-pincher, keep your sense of humour intact. Remember that you will become somebody else's nut case, and some of your friends will have many a giggle, but it's your wallet that has to pay all the bills, not theirs. Be a happy nut case.

Be happy in the knowledge that your self-reliance and thrift are contributing to being environmentally friendly, and this has become much more acceptable than it was when we took our decisions in the early 60s to avoid chemicals, poisons and waste of fuels.

You do not have to have a battery of cleaners to keep a house clean! Many of them are quite dangerous. Washing-up liquid, vinegar and bicarbonate of soda are mild, but powerful cleaners. Choose a dry powder, such as own-brand 'floor and wall cleaner', which you can mix in varying proportions according to the cleaning job you're doing. If you read the list of ingredients, you'll find bicarbonate of soda is one of the main constituents anyway. Washing-up liquid and water works on every kind of plastic known (to me, at least), and not much of either of them – just a slightly damp cloth.

## No home should be without it

Vinegar is the environment's and the penny pincher's friend, both as cleaner and disinfectant. You can wipe cupboards and bread bins with a vinegar-soaked cloth to help prevent mould!

The best shower-door cleaner is white vinegar. Wipe it on, leave to soak for a few minutes if the door has disappeared under a layer of white gunge, then rinse it well, use a squeegee blade, and polish dry. Impressive. Works on tiles, too.

To absorb cooking odours, put a saucer of vinegar beside the cooker. Cabbage has a way of filling the house which doesn't elicit the 'mmmmm' that bread or coffee manages.

Keep a bottle of half vinegar/half water to neutralise baby and pet puddles on carpets and furnishings instead of using expensive chemicals.

For a quick and easy air freshener, keep a spray bottle filled with half-and-half water and vinegar.

You can dispense with fabric softener (no pun intended). Vinegar is an excellent substitute, and many people are allergic to the materials used in softeners.

Clean vacuum flasks with a soak of half vinegar/half water, then rinse with clear water.

Descale the kettle by boiling up half-and-half vinegar and water solution, leave overnight, rinse – unless your kettle instructions say otherwise!

Two for the price of one: mix equal quantities of white vinegar and warm water, use to wash your windows – clean windows and soft hands.

You don't need proprietary window cleaners at all. Vinegar and water work, and even that can be skipped by using newspaper, water and elbow grease.

One word of caution: vinegar is acidic, and therefore can damage some surfaces such as marble, stone, and quarry tiles. On any surface, especially if you have used it neat, rinse well afterwards just to be sure it isn't still active.

---

Bath cleaners are not one of life's necessities. A little washing-up liquid after every use is enough.

The very best air freshener? Fresh air! Open the window for a little while – it's free. Air fresheners do not freshen air, they block your sense of smell.

Use no petrol at all for one day.

Cut down your speed from 70mph to 60mph for a petrol saving of about 15 per cent.

Wash your own car instead of using a car wash.

Share a ride to work.

Walk a mile instead of driving – not only will you save pennies, but you will feel better.

Make leisure time money-saving time. Take a walk and see how much food for free you can find. There are sloes, rosehips, blackberries and elderberries everywhere you look in the autumn, dandelions in the summer, sorrel in the spring. Know what you are looking at, though. There are excellent books available on wild edible plants around the world. Do not eat small Arctic buttercups – you will regret it. On the other hand, learn to recognise the Australian water tree, and South Africa is blessed with the stapelia. Be wary of fungi.

Buy British-grown foods in season. It isn't just being economical for yourself, it really and truly is helping the country, and ultimately back to your own wallet.

If you have to take a sweater off indoors because you're too warm, you are wasting money – turn the central heating down.

An oft-heard piece of wisdom: Turn down your central heating by one degree Centigrade and you will save approximately 8 per cent on your annual bill. (Somehow it ought to work, therefore, that if you turn it down by 10 degrees Centigrade you're almost heating for free, but who worked out 8 per cent in the first place? Starting from where?)

It doesn't always work out cheaper to run your central heating system on a time cycle, switching on and off. If the house gets cold, then has condensation, it can be more expensive to heat it back up again and you have the condensation problem as well. CHECK your fuel usage for at least a week each, first with the timed cycle as usual, then on constant BUT AT A

LOWER TEMPERATURE. Choose the cheapest way. Every house is different, every system is different. Know your own, and use it efficiently.

COLD? Before you reach for that thermostat, PUT ON A SWEATER! It's paid for – the heat isn't.

Still cold? Then DO something – vacuum, dust, make up a bed, wash a window, get some exercise somehow, and you will not only feel warm, but you will feel better, and your house will become warm and clean.

Rinse your hands in cold water. Sounds awful? Then think about it: you probably already do, but you do it under the HOT tap, turning it off before you get hot water. But you have wasted the hot water that was drawn from the cylinder and which will then go cold in the pipes while the heater works to heat up the new cold water which filled the cylinder.

Two or even three lightweight sweaters are warmer than one thick sweater.

Two pairs of tights (or socks if you're a chap) are much, much warmer than one.

More for the girls: keep your winter skirts long – mini skirts make maxi thighs!

If you're sitting still, wrap an afghan or small blanket around your shoulders. If you are writing, or something similar, you will find that fingerless gloves are warm and cosy.

At night, keep warm by wearing bedsocks – and remember all the old pictures of people wearing nightcaps? You lose more heat from the top of your head than anywhere else.

Sleep with wool underneath you – a fleece if you have it, or you could use an old felted sweater.

Close doors to rooms that you don't use – keep them cool. Keep the heat where it's needed.

Close the curtains at night to help keep heat inside.

Pine cones burn.

Food goes on cooking for several minutes after you turn off the source of heat. Therefore, turn off sources of heat a few minutes early – 365 days of several minutes' saved energy mount up.

Hot water costs more than cold water. Not everybody knows this, so now you do if you didn't.

Change a 100W light bulb to a 60W one which costs 60 per cent as much to operate.

Use no electricity at all for one day. Of course, don't throw a switch if you have a freezer! By the end of the day you'll undoubtedly have an inkling about how much entertainment eats into your budget.

Instead of watching TV, read something … anything. Cereal boxes or junk mail if you have to … or get out that sketch pad you 'haven't had time to use'.

Turn off unnecessary lights. It's all right to use electricity, but not to WASTE it.

Read your electricity meter once a week – write it down. After about three weeks you should see a pattern. Now change that pattern. Downwards.

Last one out TURN OUT THE LIGHTS.

Is anyone watching the TV?

Save a small fortune by 1) giving up smoking, and 2) not using the expensive nicotine gums but chewing a little bit of beeswax instead.

Use bicarbonate of soda as a deodorant (but note that it is not an antiperspirant): wash with warm water and soap, sprinkle about half a teaspoon bicarb into your hand, make a solution with more water, apply with a damp face cloth. It works. Bicarbonate of soda has an absolute multitude of uses! One of the best deodorants ever, nonallergenic, cheaper, a superb cleaning material ... what more does one want?

If you doubt the efficacy of bicarbonate of soda, just try sprinkling a bit in your shoes.

Non-iron, permanent press fabric is a modern miracle. The Americans have unsurpassable ones which come through the tumble dryer without needing 'touching up' with the iron.

It costs nothing to wash a few cloth table napkins in a load of laundry, especially if you've chosen a non-iron fabric. Consider the price of paper napkins, and how much more civilised are cloth ones.

'Let the little one's clothes be always spotlessly clean, neat and well-fitting, but remember that the more simply a child is dressed the better she will look, whilst an over-dressed child will invariably lay her parents open to the charge of vulgarity.' *The Woman's Book,* 1911.

So these, then, are the beginnings of living better for less by looking at self-reliance, thrift, environmental friendliness. None of them are difficult. All of them can be done quietly.

# 2

# What New Technology Can Do for You

*An ounce of achievement beats a ton of entertainment.*

It is said that when you buy a brand new computer, it is already out of date – they are working on the newest state-of-the-art, high-tech and really expensive models.

The joy of electronic devices is that they are highly reliable and can last a long time. But the problem with electronic devices is that they can last forever. Your old Sinclair computer may still be as good as the day you bought it, but it is way out of date because it probably doesn't do enough for you now and is unlikely to be worth any repairs. Is it time for an update?

Is your mobile phone three years old? Is it really thin, does it take photos, and does it flip open? No, but does it, the one you have already paid for, do everything you want in the way of communications? If it has all the features you need, then updating is a sign that you are becoming a fashion victim. Sad, really.

New technology is particularly fast-moving in communications – telephones changed very little for seventy years or so and now each innovation is dated before you finish dialing the number.

Modern communications have changed our lives, and made working from home possible, at the same time reducing travel time and costs. A home office can fit into what estate agents call 'deceptively spacious' cupboards, with the world at the flick of a switch. If you travel a lot on business, a laptop is a tiny piece of power.

Much of 'new technology' is 'new entertainment' with 'must-haves' wanted not only by those who buy them but by thieves as well!

We do live in a fast-moving world, but it always has been that way, the trick is trying to keep up-to-date enough to avoid being an old fogey but without becoming a shopping freak.

Some of our favourite money-savers – Mercury, mill end shops, faxing everything we could – have disappeared or moved abroad or become outmoded in only a few years, and some of today's new tech will be tomorrow's junk.

Prices drop fairly quickly on high-tech gadgets! It is quite unlikely that you really MUST HAVE the newest – let others buy the prestige goods, you take the time to evaluate the value-for-money aspect. Buy TOOLS not TOYS.

Computers are wonderful money savers, or big time wasters.

Many suppliers, especially airlines, give a discount for booking online.

Email beats postage stamps any day.

Google, or one of the other search machines, is a wonderful place to start hunting for recipes, spare parts, and everything you ever wanted to know, and much that you didn't.

Most computers come with Excel, or a similar spreadsheet package, already installed, and there you have the framework for keeping track of income and expenditure.

The pain of buying university textbooks can be lessened by buying new or used ones online at very considerable savings.

Computer monitors make excellent film screens if you want to hire a film on DVD, and have a small audience, say, just the two of you. Make your own popcorn.

Flat screen monitors get full marks.

If you are writing a book, like this one, then it has to be typed on a computer, or the publishers probably would not look at it.

Good printers that also do copying and are fax machines and scanners, are remarkably cheap. How do they do that? By making their ink amazingly expensive, so you pay for the printer when buying ink refills. This is a very old marketing trick, and it is said that Texaco gave away oil lamps in the 1920s to the Chinese, thereby creating a market for Texaco oil. So buy the printer, and then you can go online to find alternative ink sources.

If you want to print a longish thing, say 20 pages, and your printer is saying the ink is low, you can probably fool it into NOT stopping mid-task by doing the job in stages, say 4 or 5 pages at a time – printers aren't THAT smart, it will think it has ink enough for small runs. If the ink is really low, it will stop.

Newspapers are bulky, expensive and loaded with advertising. Try the same newspaper online. Most of them are free.

Once cash gets into a pocket, it seems that all that money wants to do is be free! It sneaks out, leaks out, sticks to hands in a most insidious way and escapes. The only way to stop cash disappearing is to pay bills by email or post, and leave cash where it belongs, in a bank.

Shopping online at a supermarket can make sense, if you are very busy, and at least you are not tempted by products on the shelves which aren't on the shopping list.

EBay is already an institution and most people have had only good experiences with it. Next time you need batteries for a watch, mobile phone, torch or any other gadget, try eBay. New or old, there may a bargain there. Our neighbour has bought a second-hand Rayburn kitchen range on eBay for £46.

CAD – computer aided design – is here to stay, and can be used for everything from gardens and houses to embroidery and clothes patterns. There are plenty of experts out there who will do it for you, or you can sit down and teach yourself.

Same with desk-top publishing – make your own birthday and other special occasion cards, launch a neighbourhood newspaper, or help out on a church or political newsletter.

Sometimes it takes perseverance to use new technology – the first time I ever sat down to try a word processor, I flicked a few switches and two big words came up on the screen: Fatal Error.

Digital cameras are replacing film cameras, and now wildlife photographers and people who require great detail in their photographs are using them. Photographs can be transferred to a CD or DVD or put onto slides for projectors and many will never be printed, saving film development costs.

You can also make your own computer screen savers from your digital photos.

Should you have only a few digital prints to make, it is probably cheapest to take the camera to a print shop for them to produce the chosen pictures, but desk-top printers are getting better all the time and special papers are available to produce excellent prints.

Mobile phones are very nice to have if you are making a car journey at night. It also helps if you have remembered to put the phone number of your breakdown service in the car and in the mobile.

Text messages are wonderfully cheap, especially if you want to use your phone on the Continent to contact friends at home.

Answering machines are useful in business but at home why promise to call people back on your money? If they want to talk to you they'll ring again.

New technology has enabled telesales centres to be even more irritating than they previously were, by calling ten or more numbers at the same time. The telesales person talks to the first one who answers, HANGING UP on all the others. It was amusing to read that when this first started happening neighbours were going over and beating each other to a pulp thinking it was pest calls.

Telesales calls can be dealt with by not answering the phone straight away as it may be one of THEM. Register to have your number removed from telesales lists. Never use callback if they leave a number – it could be very expensive – but almost always they withhold THEIR number. If you do get a telesales call, HANG UP ON THEM.

Not everything new under the sun is new – just more widely available now. Remember when all telephones were rented from the GPO? General Post Office. Post office and telephones all one word, nationalised and what was that word customer? Now we can all toddle down to Sainsbury's and buy our own phones for very low prices, and cordless telephones are at least convenient, though that little red light means it is always using power.

Speaking of little red lights, sometimes things are invented, and later comes a use for them! In about 1964 we were at the Detroit Boat Show and a huge crowd had gathered around one of the fringe stands, fascinated by a piece of machinery about the size of a lathe, consisting of a row of numbers, glowing red and marking time – the seconds and minutes were easy to keep up with; it was the tenths, hundredths, thousandths and beyond that held everybody's attention, with the last numbers on the right not visibly changing, but you could see all ten digits glowing. The charming two or three young men who had invented the device kept saying, yeah, it's fun, but nobody can think of anything to do with it! LED.

Paper shredders have become popular as a good way of handling old bank statements and all those things that identity thieves want to get hold of, and the end product makes a fine cat litter, but burning is a better way of dealing with the disposal problem if you can do fire. Or turn the stuff into papier mâché and save electricity.

New technology can be skill-killing, too, especially in the DIY field. Nail guns and power saws are formidable tools, but the 'craftsmen' who use them are soon unable to use a hammer or saw AT ALL.

Sewing machines can now do amazing embroidery – at vast cost – and probably about as much fun as sitting on an assembly line watching a robot riveter. Don't buy more technology than you need!

We don't have satellite navigation in our car, old fogies that we are, but it's a lot of fun to be in the children's cars and listen to robot lady patronisingly breathing 'make a U-turn at the earliest possible opportunity' just because we suddenly turned off to look at something interesting. SatNav has been getting bad press, though, because of diverting traffic down quiet country lanes, and that is a really bad thing to be doing.

The TV also goes for a ride with many families, the kids strapped in the back seat all according to latest regulations, a flickering screen in front of them. Whatever happened to 'I spy with my little eye …'

So not all new technology is good. Information overload? Just because it's on a website doesn't make it true. Be critical – just as when you see or hear 'new studies show…' ask 'Who said?' 'Who sponsored the study?' 'Who stands to gain by it?'

Nor, it must be said, is all technology bad! We live in today's world, not yesterday's. While not strictly essential for survival, a food processor does a better job at cakes than by hand, and at lightning speed as well. At 650 watts, it is almost difficult to calculate the cost of using it for making pastry – it runs for less than 35 seconds.

Newer boilers with heat condensers are supposed to be very efficient, but before throwing out the old boiler, ask if it is past its best. Our oil boiler is at least 20 years old, and the very good serviceman says that it is as efficient as anything available now, and better made than new ones.

Neither TVs nor computers benefit from being left on standby, as they did a few years ago. All such equipment can be turned off, just like well-organised households turn off lights when not in use. Equipment on standby may be using 1/3rd the power of being on, but nobody is benefiting except the power companies.

If 'cheap' is important to you above all, then supermarket bread is a very good purchase, may the Lord have mercy on your tum. However, a bread machine is a way of matching long-term economy and better living. It does mean thinking ahead, setting timers and making sure you have all your ingredients. By using the delay button, hard-grained granary flour can soak overnight and you can save a lot in dental costs.

Microwaves have been around a long time, but they have still managed to improve, and they are the most efficient in terms of energy usage for cooking, and they fit around a busy schedule. The cost of microwaves is now so low that they are good economic sense.

Small counter-top ovens are super, using less energy than large conventional ovens, and now you can find them combined with microwaves. There have been very few new developments in ovens over the last several decades, but this is one that is not half bad.

'Build a better mousetrap …' or a better range of kitchen tools! Not the must-have die-for gadgets, but the lowly potato peeler, tin opener, garlic press and such with comfortable handles and business ends that REALLY WORK. Worth every penny, so far lasting for several years.

Microfibre cloth has arrived for cleaning things – and with no chemicals! Only water – we like that a lot. The first ones we saw were the ones with new eyeglasses. Now everybody is selling cloths, mops, fabric, sports clothes, baby nappies, you name it, all kinds of textures. They work best when new.

A modern miracle is the fleece throw. These now cost almost nothing, wash beautifully and dry almost instantly. Wrap up in one or two of these and who needs central heating and fossil fuels? Fleece fabric for dressing gowns, blankets, house slippers … a real innovation.

We have watched with amusement as razor blades changed from the old so-called safety razor which needed only a few pieces of loo paper stuck to the wounds, through dual blades promising eternal beauty, and reckon triple blades really do work! Will they go on adding another row of sharp steel every year or so? Do kids still sneak their dad's razor to shave Action Man? Does he come with his own miniature kit?

Aren't battery-operated toothbrushes great? We thought they were just about the most ridiculous things we'd heard of until the children and grandchildren kept recommending them. A special offer at Sainsbury's and we've never looked back – you want the ones with two brushes that reciprocate. Shorter brushes, too, take very little toothpaste!

It would be a mistake to forgo either the old-fashioned or the new-fangled just because of its being old or new. Our ideal is to use the best of each, whichever gives us true value for money. Better for less, whether old and comforting, or new and daunting.

Interestingly, we have found that no one really knows how long CDs will last – not in popularity, but actually, physically, retain the information stored on them! They're mostly beet juice or similar. DVDs are the flavour of the moment, but something will replace those as well. Thus we progress. Don't throw away the paper and pencil just yet.

# 3

# Intelligent Shopping

To know what you prefer, instead of humbly saying Amen to what the world tells you you ought to prefer, is to have kept your soul alive.

ROBERT LOUIS STEVENSON, AN INLAND VOYAGE

We buy things we do not need, and when we get them home we do not enjoy them. Worse, when we get them home, they make us miserable because we know we shouldn't have bought them, and we then have to make other sacrifices to pay for something we didn't need.

Shops know how to manipulate us. They have been studying us for years and they have run those studies through their computers so that they can encourage us to buy more than we had intended. They know where we look when we go into a store. They know what colours attract us. They stack their shelves so that we have to bend down to pick up a staple item and our eyes will drift over expensive ones ... so ... WHY DON'T WE STUDY THEM AND USE THAT STUDY TO OUR OWN ADVANTAGE.

This is not a chapter on where to shop – it's about thinking and planning before you shop. There's an easy way to save lots of money every year – you must be willing to think about WHY you are about to buy something. Is it because you need or want it, or have you been enticed into buying it? Do you want to buy it, not for yourself, but for someone dear to you to show that you love them? A large percentage of purchases is made by women, and marketing and advertising appeal to the altruistic guilt of women – from the instant food that needs something added so she doesn't feel she's cheating her family, to the clever packaging that makes her feel the product inside is a symbol of her love and a symbol of the virility of her loved one! One fashion-industry man back in 1950 made the famous comment, 'it is our job to make women unhappy with what they have …'

Write out a list of what you need to buy before you go shopping. Clutch this list in your fat little paw. Do not leave it on the sideboard or on the desk. Take it with you, refer to it often, and resist the temptation to buy something you see that isn't NEEDED. Leave room to write next to each item how much you paid, as this helps you remember how much things cost, and forms a record for future comparisons.

Keep a list of staples – things that you buy every time you go into the grocery shop or that you always keep in stock; treat these as 'impulse' buys if you see them on special even if they aren't on your shopping list for that trip.

A shopping list is not a command, it is a guideline, a plan. Be ready to change it at a moment's notice, say if you went in to buy a pork roast and the shop is having a special on fish, switch menus around to buy cheap fish instead that week.

Do compare prices of the same items between shops – you're supposed to choose the lower one, by the way, but always aim for best quality at best price.

The wear and tear on your time, your nerves, on petrol for the car, make it almost impossible for the busy man or woman to do a comparison shop for every item. There are other things in life a lot more fun than shopping. You only have to do a comparison shop once, or at least, only once in a while.

No shop is best for everything. They all work on 'swings and roundabouts' and if one thing is cheap, then another has to be expensive. You have to know who has the good bacon, who has the good cheese, who has the good beef. Make more lists.

Never go grocery shopping when you are hungry – eat something, anything, otherwise everything looks delicious and smells wonderful, and you buy more than you had intended.

Big tins are usually cheaper per unit of contents, but check first. Those little bits of information on shelf or label giving price per unit or weight can be very useful to you.

The 'own-brand' product is almost always straight out of a brand-product factory, usually cheaper and often better than other branded goods. Glance around at the nearby branded products, and if own-label and branded have the same container, you can probably guess who made the own-label product.

Buy an own-label instant coffee instead of a brand name one. Buy a large tin of instant coffee instead of several small jars over several weeks. The difference in price is substantial – sometimes. But you will know, because you have checked the fine print on the shelf price tag and have seen the price per unit!

If there isn't much difference in the unit price or the quality of the coffee then buy the one with the tin or jar that you want to keep peanuts in.

Usually supermarkets are cheaper than the corner shop, but not if you let yourself yield to every temptation they dangle before you – and they are experts at that!

Supermarkets are almost always more expensive for fresh foods than local greengrocers or butchers.

Many readers of the *Penny Pincher Paper* have a very efficient way of dealing with supermarkets. They have a competition with themselves as to how fast they can get in, buy what they came for, and get out again. Some of them even have a map of the store, so they can plot the most efficient path through.

Loose vegetables are cheaper than plastic-wrapped ones. You do already know that, don't you? If this piece of information comes as a surprise to you, you have got a real shopping problem.

Unless you are AT Wimbledon, don't buy strawberries during Wimbledon.

While taking advantage of specials on items you keep all the time, don't stock up with huge quantities of anything expensive unless you know you WILL use it all before it swells up, turns black, and dies.

Here is an interesting exercise. Look around and find someone selling potatoes in large bags (28 lbs/12 Kg or bigger). Then buy a packet of crisps, note the weight, and now divide that weight into the weight of the big bag of potatoes, and then multiply the price of the bag of crisps by that number. Got it? That is how much you are paying to have potatoes processed into crisps. Crisps are a really expensive way to eat potatoes.

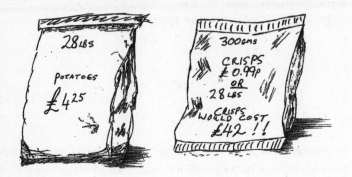

Buying a large bag of potatoes may mean that you can't use them all, but it is still cheaper to throw away/give away/trade the excess than to buy a smaller bag at a higher price per unit. Large bags of potatoes are not expensive.

Or you can use big-business practices when buying things – JIT: Just In Time. Why should you tie up your money and fill up your shelf space with products that will still be in the shop the day before you need it – especially if you're passing the shop every day? If it is good enough for big business, it is good enough for you.

One product may be cheaper, but will it last as long? Silicon baking paper costs more than greaseproof, but silicon can be used over and over again.

'Best before' means that the product is at its peak before that date, but 'use before' means that it is probably safer to do just that. Medicines have 'use before' dates that should be stuck to. Many cheeses are just getting palatable by their 'best before' date.

Lots of containers like mayonnaise or peanut butter jars leave easily 5% of the contents stuck to the bottom or sides when emptied, so have a flexible plastic spatula to hand to get every last bit out. It is just the same as having a 5% price reduction.

Double your saving: say no to children whining for sweets – save money on sweets and even more on dentistry. And build good character in the little tyke.

When the budget for food has gone way over the top, look through what is in the shopping bag, and the chances are that there are more 'convenience' foods than there are 'real' foods and staple items such as flour, margarine and milk.

Open patterns of china are meant to be open forever, so that you can add to your set or replace plates that get broken. Live in the expectation that the pattern you choose will close three weeks after you purchase, so it may be a good idea to get used to mix and match sets.

Once while on holiday in Scotland there was on the bed a blanket with the date of purchase sewn in. It was dated 1926. Whatever the original price, that was a good buy. Buying quality pays off.

Very small spiral notebook from 'name' office-supply shop £1.89. Large spiral notebook from small newsagent 42p.

As manufacturing moves out of Britain, there are fewer mill shops and factory shops available, and it makes sense to look at secondhand outlets for well-made goods. Help your favourite charities, reduce waste and pollution, and save money all in one go.

The man who has enough tools has yet to be born, so check out car boot sales and jumble sales. Buy only from stallholders who do not look as though they have used one of the tools to gain possession from a former owner.

Use the old three-purse trick … not separate purses, but one purse inside another and your money is in the little one down inside the other two. While struggling to get your money out you may decide you don't want to spend it after all.

Does a half-price sale mean that something is a bargain? Possibly, but first, do you want it at all? Even at half-price is it more expensive than the same thing at another shop? Why didn't it sell at full price? Perhaps it is of poor quality, or it is just downright ugly.

A bargain is not a bargain unless you need it, and if a bargain is too good to be true, it probably isn't true.

Men's shoes are best old and comfortable. If you need black shoes to go with business suits, then the choice is between buying at a discount centre and they will be good value, lasting several years. Or, paying for a really good pair that will last years and years, getting more comfortable all the time. That is also economical.

Children outgrow shoes in a matter of months and the quality of the shoe has little effect on children's feet, for all they need is shoes that are big enough for growing feet. Look for shoes that are practical for walking and are cheap.

Women's shoes. Well, what can you say?

Window-shopping can be good if it is really comparison shopping. But if it is the path of temptation, leading to buying what you cannot really afford, then be sure to limit your window-shopping to times when the shop door is firmly shut. Window-shopping should give you 'inspirations of your own – not aspirations to *own.*'

Credit cards are most useful. They let you buy over the phone, there is no need to carry cash around, avoiding theft and helping thrift, and many purchases by card will give an added level of guarantee. If the balance is paid off in full every month, then they are an assistant to good money management, but the interest rates charged on credit balances are very high, often above 20%. Only the rich can afford to pay credit card interest rates, and they don't need credit cards.

If you have to use credit cards, at least try to use them for things that will still be around when you finish paying for them.

Shops change over time, so the shop that, say, was cheapest for toiletries last year, may not be such a good deal this year. In fact, shops can be quite sneaky, setting low prices when they come into the market, and then slowly raising their prices. Remember, the interests of the shop are not the interests of the buyer. They are trying to get the highest price, or at least, trying to get the biggest profit over time, that they can.

If you buy books over the internet, don't forget the postage. In fact it may be cheaper to buy books from the local library when they have their sale, or from charity shops or book fairs.

Hunting for the book you want in second-hand bookshops is a hobby in itself. All the Patrick O'Brian naval books with John Aubrey as the hero, for instance, and you have to buy them in sequence.

All great literature is there in second-hand bookshops, often in beautiful binding and illustrated. Not every book in a charity shop will be 1967 road atlases or be written by Catherine Cookson, bless her.

Do you really know your local markets? Going around a market is entertainment in itself, and you will be doing your pocketbook a favour by buying vegetables there, and clothes, and luggage, and garden plants, and … Prices can drop dramatically about the time the traders close up. If you keep your wits about you, you can live well out of a market.

If you are slightly crumbly around the edges, as we are, you need to know which shops are giving pensioners 10% or more off on which days.

If you have planned your shopping, then your purchases will last until the next time you have to go out. That saves money on bus fares and car parking, and keeps you away from temptation.

If you buy something that was not on your list but you really do need, then make a note to get it on the list next time. With practice, you will be able to make better lists.

Buy only what you need, but buy enough so that it will last you until the next shopping trip – you aren't saving money if you're always popping into the shops to top up supplies.

Learn to say – to yourself at least – 'I can't afford that item'. All of us want things we will never be able to afford, so just acknowledge that you cannot have it and move on to something else. (That Rembrandt will never grace my walls, sigh).

Advertisers would have you believe that you deserve the very best, and also the most expensive. Are the advertisers working for you or for the seller?

Local newspapers and car boot sales are tricky. There are wonderful bargains, but it is easy to find that the bargains, wonderful as they are, are not actually needed.

Now auctions are a great way to save money – and to lose money. 'Buyer beware' is the rule at auctions. You have very few rights if the item does not look so good when you get it home. Have a good look, and then set your top limit. It is so easy to get competitive when bidding against some old crone in the corner, but let her have it, if she wants to pay that much.

The Post Office puts up the price of stamps about once a year, and then all the stamps in the house are a penny or two too little, and then you have to buy more stamps. Instead, ask for First or Second class stamps that have no price on them, but the Post Office will honour them for years.

You probably know that laundry detergents these days have visual brighteners in them that do nothing to clean clothes, but just make them look brighter. Don't pay extra for products that make your clothes glow in the dark!

Shop first with pen and paper, then with the phone and Yellow Pages, and finally with your wallet.

Internet shopping can be quick, easy … and expensive. Take care.

Don't fall victim to the words 'environmentally friendly' either! It easily means 'our profit'. You can spend a lot on a tin crusher or you can jump up and down on it for free.

Watch out for wish words. These are words crafted by very clever people in advertising departments that are focused on your psyche, and they have studied how to hit us: words like 'luxurious', 'you owe it to yourself', 'specially crafted', 'charm', 'graceful', 'fragrant', 'distinctive', and many another word that will tempt the unwary shopper.

Shopping is a contest of wills. The shop wants to sell you something you don't need for as much as possible, and you want to buy what you do need at the lowest price possible. As long as each side respects the other's position, shopping can be a successful and pleasant (well, not too bad) experience.

'Shopping therapy' is bad news. It is like taking a drink to clear a hangover. Going shopping to feel better, to comfort yourself, is for the weak and insecure. You are strong and secure, and you are out to win.

Let's be fair to shops. We need them, and they, or most of them, try to give us a nice ambience for shopping, and to have an attractive selection of products on the shelves. They try to give good value for money, we try to get excellent value for money.

There are two ways to go shopping: we can go looking for bargains, or we can hunt out value for money, and we all do both. Isn't it satisfying when we get a real bargain?

# 4

# DIY – You Really Can Do It

*Cease to use your hands, and you have lopped off a huge chunk of your consciousness.*

GEORGE ORWELL

Just because you cannot do all of a job does not mean you cannot do any of it. If you want an extension on the house, you may know that bricklaying is beyond you, but that does not mean you cannot find out how big a trench is needed for the foundations and dig that yourself.

Glue a piece of felt to the bottom of a 6″ square ceramic tile to make a heat-resistant mat.

Save as much wood scraps as you can for repairs, making door wedges, or children's toys. When the scraps get too small, use them on the barbecue, and then put the ash on flower beds.

Mix sawdust with wood glue to make tight dowel joints or to repair furniture.

You can make your own 'plastic wood' as you need it by mixing fine sawdust with a synthetic glue. Either add dry pigment to match the colour of the piece you are repairing, or use a piece of the same wood to create the sawdust.

If appearances are not important, then cover single-glazed windows with plastic sheeting. It is cheap and gives most of the benefits in terms of heat loss as the expensive double glazing. You may be able to find a plastic sheet converter who will sell you seconds.

If an item is broken and you cannot get it repaired, or the repairs are too expensive compared to the cost of buying a new one, then have a go at fixing it yourself. If your repair fails you are no worse off, and you may have learned something that will lead to success in a future repair.

Make up your own pastes, glues and play doughs using salt, flour and water.

Paint a wall rather than wallpaper it – the difference in cost is substantial, and you can see what is going on with the wall. Wallpaper may hide a multitude of sins, but it also hides problems that you ought to be monitoring.

Wooden toys are hard to find now, because they are so expensive, so make wooden toys yourself. Remember those scraps of wood we saved?

You can make artificial flowers from florists' wire and nylon tights. While I personally wouldn't stick them in a vase, they can be fun as a gift bow, or you could tuck some into a fun hat. Children enjoy making them.

Chopped up tights and stockings make a washable stuffing for soft toys and last forever.

Weddings are one of those times money just leaks out of your pocket to caterers, marquee suppliers, dressmakers and many more. If you plan ahead, you can make the dress, prepare the food, ice the wedding cake, and book the village hall, and save thousands. You may go grey.

Decorate Easter eggs by using onion skins and flowers and vegetables from the garden and hedgerows for colour – wet the eggs (white ones work best), press a few flower petals on, wrap with the outer, brown onion skins for a 'gilded' look, secure with strips of cloth, string, or even rubber bands. Try some without the onion skins for other colours. Add vegetables and fruits from the garden or freezer to boiling water, then drop in the egg mummies and hardboil. Spinach, beetroot, blackberries, damsons, gorse blossom all give beautiful colours. No two are ever alike.

Make tiny baubles for the Christmas tree from a gaudy, large, shiny necklace (jumble sales and charity shops will have them). String a large bead with two or three small ones and hang on the tree with a paperclip.

Recognise your limits – in time, money and talents. If you don't know enough about electricity to change a plug, then you would be pretty daft to set about re-wiring a house. But your friendly electrician, at £100 a day, sometime, way back when, began by learning how to change a plug. Once you have learnt how to do that, then learn a little more, provided the wretched Health and Safety people have not ruled that we are not allowed to do it anymore.

Marble mantles went out of fashion many years ago, so they got painted over. Marble, like any natural material, is a pretty material, but it can easily be ruined. Carefully scrape off the paint and use no chemicals. Get the last bits out with fine wire wool (0000 grade). Polish with beeswax-turpentine furniture polish. Do not ever be tempted to clean with anything acidic (and that includes of course, lemon and vinegar).

Rain water damages walls, so at least once a year go all round the outside of the house with a ladder, checking the gutters for blockages and damage.

The first resource for the budding car mechanic/plumber/decorator is the local library, but you may want to learn more. Try the courses offered by your local college and take a full course, if you have time. You will find yourself competing with bright 16-year olds, but they are good courses.

Cracks and holes in plasterboard can be repaired using ready-mixed tubs of plaster, and then sand down to get a flat finish, before painting over. It is a bit like icing a Christmas cake, only slower.

Decide whether a repair has to be a professional one and it needs to be done right now, or whether it could be a DIY hold-it-together-for-a-while one. Just as a plaster may be enough on a wound instead of having to have stitches – the same is true about many a job where the repairman called in will suck in his breath sharply and suggest your house will fall down before sunset unless you sign up right now for him to mend the downpipe. Give yourself time to assess what is really needed right now, and more time to do a good repair later.

Wood pallets that are not to a standard size have no commercial value, but they could be useful as a source of wood building materials to you. John built an entire stable from second-hand pallets, including making a 'tiled' roof, hanging each 'tile' by a reclaimed nail. As we say in our family 'There's no point in throwing money at a problem.'

Sometimes building materials can be had for free. If you see a tumbledown shed that you could turn into a good fence or gate, the shed owner may be grateful to you for taking it away (ASK FIRST). You'll have to use some elbow grease, but it won't cost a lot of money. Our brother and his wife collected all the bricks to build a house from old chimney stacks and decrepit buildings lurking around the countryside, hauled them home and hand-cleaned every one of them, but that's a bargain price for a house.

When doing a repair job using cement, it is worth taking the time to make a calculation of how much cement you need for the work. There is nothing worse than to nearly complete the patch and then run out, or to have half the mix left over, which is a waste. One is tempted to make garden gnomes of this residue, and that is always a mistake.

## Paint

Odds and ends of paint can be mixed as long as they are of the same type – i.e. emulsion or oil – and have your own designer colours. Just don't run out halfway round the room!

Once a tin of paint has been opened air will slowly penetrate even a closed tin, forming that thick skin on top of the paint. If you are bold, then turn the tin upside down, or if you are chicken-hearted, then shake the tin to coat the inside of the lid with wet paint. That will seal out the air.

Professional painters buy good-quality paint brushes as they can load them with paint and use them effectively, but most DIYers are not that good. The amateur painter is often better off pennywise to buy really cheap brushes when a job has to be done and then throw the brush away, rather than clean the brush thoroughly with white spirit that might cost as much as a new brush.

Don't let your brush go hard and gungy while you are on your coffee break. Just slip a plastic bag or film over the brush head and wrap it around to keep out air. Brushes can safely be left overnight this way. An alternative is to put the brush wet with paint into a tin of water.

Use small tins for paint instead of dipping your brush into the big tin. You will waste less paint on the small tin than you will by letting the big tin dry out or get dirty. Also, if you drop the wretched tin it is not quite such a disaster.

Paintbrushes used with emulsion paint should be washed out with soap and water, while brushes used with oil paint need to be cleaned right after use with white spirit, and then the brushes should be left to dry without crumpling the hairs. Wrap them firmly with newspaper while they are still slightly damp to keep their shape. Somehow not all brushes get the full treatment and most households have brushes that are as hard as a rock, or brushes that have sat in turpentine so long that it is surrounded by a sticky jelly. Yes, you can buy brush restorers, but brushes today are so cheap that it is better to use the old brushes as fire lighters.

Put on rubber gloves and then a pair of old gloves or use a rag, dip into the paint pot and anywhere you can reach you can paint – try it on pipework, etc.

The most important feature of a good paint job is how well that first coat, the primer, sticks to the bare wood or metal, so, buy the best primer paint that you can afford, and then save money on the undercoat and top coat. After putting on that good primer, the next most important factor in a long-lasting paint job is the thickness of the paint.

———

Decorating can only do so much to conceal the real features of a room. An eight-foot square room won't become any more spacious by painting it a cool colour. The only way you can make an eight-foot square room more spacious is by moving the walls. You can give a bit of an illusion of space with a light blue colour, but you still have an eight-foot square room, so don't try to recreate the Sistine chapel in it.

Colour schemes, curtains, furniture, all are subject to fashion, and trying to keep up with the ideas of the many home decorating magazines is going to cost a fortune. This year's ravishing peach is next year's out-of-date yucky orange. But look around your neighbourhood and just count the number of houses that are being extended and redecorated. It is the national sport, and the habitat of the DIYer.

You don't have to buy everything you see in a glossy magazine – as you thumb through the scrumptious decorating/house magazine, look at everything with a new eye: what can you make? Which things that you admire do you already have, or have something similar?

Even a kitchen can be transformed without spending a fortune: if your cupboards are still good, why not just change the doors? There are specialist firms that will do this for you, but if you are at all handy you can do it for a fraction of the cost. It is now very easy to find professional fittings, much easier than it was twenty years ago when we made our own kitchen fittings from wood and laminate.

If you do make your own kitchen furniture, remember that you can always paint wooden cupboards a different colour if you want to change later.

You can buy a wallpaper pasting table, or take two old tea-chests and put a flush door on top. Of course, your chests and door will be a lot steadier than the bought one.

Make your own efficient, long-lasting and portable bookcase: all you need are bricks and boards. The method is simple: stack 'em.

You can make your own rugs, whether from a kit or from scraps. One of the most elegant rugs I have ever seen was a tapestry one, in a stately home. On the floor, not on a wall. If you have the patience, making a tapestry rug could be fun, but quicker is a rag rug, and this does not have to look scrappy either; you can make very pretty and practical ones with narrow strips of woollen fabric.

Replace/repair broken air bricks. For some strange reason a hole in an air brick will attract a small bird who, having got in, will be quite unable to get out without the assistance of human beings, hammers, saws, etc.

Used roofing tiles can be half the price of new tiles, and they are essential if you are making a repair to an old roof. New tiles will stand out even after years of weathering. Some care is required, because old tiles were made by many small manufacturers, and they all manufactured to their own designs and size, even when making the same type of tile. Tiles from different manufacturers will not necessarily fit neatly together. The only reliable way of getting matching tiles is to get them from a single demolition site. Ask their origin if buying from an architectural recovery yard.

Energy output from an oil-fired boiler or from an electric fire can be given in either kW or BTUs. To convert from kWs to

BTUs, multiply by 3412, and this is useful if you have made your calculations in kWs and the new boiler is rated in BTUs.

## Keeping warm for next to nothing

If you are extending your central heating system, think about whether it needs to be in every room. For instance, if you have an attic guest room, it is probably cheaper to warm it up with an electric fire for the few days of winter when guests are using it than to run central heating up there, just for the comfort of the spiders and mice.

Temperature control valves on every radiator are real money-savers, if you turn down the heat in unused rooms where it is not needed. For instance, if you are not going to use the dining room today, turn the control valve right down.

Do not be afraid to turn off the heat in a room, even in really cold weather. Some heat will still reach the room from central heating pipes, keeping it above freezing. BUT, if in doubt, leave a little heat on, as a burst pipe can cause the most awful damage to the floor and cost thousands.

Where there is a hot water pipe running through parts of the house that do not need to be heated, or where heat can be detrimental, such as through larders, then this heat can be saved for rooms that need it by lagging the pipes with foam insulation from DIY shops.

Central heating systems should be protected from corrosion by the addition of inhibitors to the central heating tank. If you have to drain this tank down, don't forget to renew the inhibitor.

Solid-fuel boilers may or may not be cheap to run, but they do produce a lot of ash that has to be cleaned up. Cinders can be used as foundation material for paths, while wood ash can go on the garden. Gooseberries love wood ash.

The old-fashioned radiator is extremely efficient at transmitting heat to a room. Even if you are installing a new, efficient central heating boiler, why not keep the old radiators?

If a radiator is fitted under a window, make sure the curtains are short enough and do not lead all the heat up the inside next to the glass, but allow the heat out into the room.

Edge the thermostat down slowly. If you reduce it drastically, the rest of the family will notice. But the rest of the family are not dim, and they will slowly edge the thermostat up again, hoping you will not be aware of their sneaky, underhand, deceitful conduct.

I have never found anyone who was really satisfied with central heating from off-peak electricity, except the people on TV who advertise the system. On the other hand, it is cheap to install.

If air gets into a central heating radiator it can cause an air lock, effectively cutting out that radiator from the system. Air locks are quite usual when a new system is installed, or the system has been drained down and refilled, but if it happens at other times, then there is an air leak somewhere that needs to be fixed. The air is bled out of the system by the little valve at the end of the radiator, using a square key made for the purpose. Bleed out all the air, until a little water appears and then turn off hard. Do not get bored and leave the air bleeding out. You will get a big puddle on the floor.

Double glazing installed by your friendly double glazing company is rarely a good investment, since the cost is high and the returns in the form of lower heating costs are spread over many years. There are additional benefits to double glazing, though, such as elimination of draughts and sound-proofing and these alone may make it well worth while to you, and future increases in fuel prices may change the cost/benefit equation and make double glazing an economic choice.

Sooner or later, usually sooner, most double glazing units mist up and need replacing.

Secondary glazing, that is, putting another sheet of glass or plastic over a window is not as efficient as vacuum-sealed double glazing units, but it is nearly as good, and much cheaper. Secondary units can be purchased, or try making your own.

Now that your house is well insulated and all the draughts have been eliminated, you will get condensation problems. Condensation is caused by warm, wet air hitting cold surfaces, and cooking, baths and breathing all create moist air, and this will cause wood to rot, and you can get unhealthy mould growing in your house. I have successfully treated this by lining walls in a bedroom with 1/8 inch (3mm) expanded polystyrene sheet, and then wallpapering over the polystyrene. This will cure those cold corners of a room that get wet and grow mould, but houses do have to be aired to be healthy.

Copper hot water tanks need efficient lagging if they are not to waste heat. Start with commercial lagging made for the size of tank you have, and then add to that with old towels, blankets and anything else you can find that will cut heat loss.

Old newspapers will burn in a fireplace, and they are not fossil fuel so they do not add to the $CO_2$ in the atmosphere. There are devices for rolling up newspapers, or you can do it by hand, and it gives good, quick, heat, but creates a lot of ash. Put the ash on the garden.

Agas, Rayburns and other kitchen ranges are not especially heat efficient for heating or cooking, but they are highly inefficient if members of your family open the oven doors to warm their backsides.

A front door and a back door lobby keep out a lot of cold wind and heat loss. If you can, close in the front and back porches, or build on, and stop that cold air sweeping in. Our front door faces North, and the enclosed lobby stays so cold for most of the year that we can use it as a secondary fridge.

A piece of Sellotape over a keyhole stops a lot of cold air blowing in. Really old doors seem to have an unreasonable number of redundant keyholes.

When you enclose the front or back door, if it catches the sun at any time of the day, it makes sense to glaze as much as possible. Even in winter the sun will turn it into a mini-greenhouse and then that heat will transfer to the main house as free heat.

Twenty per cent of the heat lost from a house is through the roof. Every roof space should be insulated with fibreglass at least four inches (100mm) thick, and six inches (150mm) is better. Fibreglass is cheap, so the cost/benefit analysis is positive for roof insulation.

When insulating the loft space, run the insulation over and around water tanks, never underneath. This way a little heat can seep up from the rooms below and keep the tanks and pipes from freezing. If a pipe does freeze, then gently warm with a butane torch or, better yet, with a hair dryer. Be prepared to turn off the main water supply, because the frozen pipe may have burst, and there is going to be a lot of water around when it is thawed out.

If you are using a butane torch, then be careful not to boil the water in the pipe, as a frozen pipe does not allow the steam to escape, and that will burst the pipe.

High winds strip heat away from a house. If you live in a windy spot, try planting trees and bushes to cut down the wind speed. The best to plant are evergreens on the windward side.

A bird nesting in the loft space is proof that there is a hole somewhere that is letting out heat. In winter a howling gale could be blowing through, so find the hole, turf the little blighters out and seal up the hole.

Underlay under a carpet not only protects the carpet and makes it more comfortable to walk on, but it also acts as an extra layer of insulation. To add even more, put down layers of old newspapers under the underlay and they will also help avoid those grey lines that appear where the floorboards don't quite meet.

Despite the cold winters in America, most houses there do not use double glazing. There is a sort of Rite of Spring every year when the detachable glass panes over the windows are removed and put into storage, and the fly screens go up. It is an easy job to make a wooden frame with glass in it, and put up hooks on the outside of the windows to hang them on. I suppose there is a Gloom of Fall, when the fly screens come down and the glass goes up.

Those little sticky strips of spongy insulation that go around doors and windows really work and are dirt cheap.

Every house needs an effective damp course. If your house does not have one, then you can hire the equipment to drill holes in the walls and inject a chemical that makes an effective water barrier. If you decide to get a contractor to do the job, get quotations and ask around for satisfied customers of this contractor. It is a field that has more than its fair share of cowboys.

Over time it is easy for earth and debris from flowerbeds to build up outside a house, lifting the soil level above the damp course. Walk around the house and look to see that this has not happened, and that the holes in all the air bricks are clear.

## Plumbing

Before calling a plumber for a dripping tap or pipe join, check to see if it is a fitting that can be tightened with a spanner. A Footprint pipewrench is a most useful tool for tightening nuts on pipes. Beware tightening too much, for brass and plastic nuts can be damaged by strong men and fragile fittings.

A surprising amount of water can get lost from a single dripping tap and most of us are on water meters now. Repair kits are cheap and the job won't take long, but do turn off the water supply first. A small leak in a plumbing system will become a big leak, if you leave it long enough.

Copper pipe water systems have joints that are either compression joints with threaded nuts, or solder joints, or both. Compression joints tend to leak more often, but they are easy

to fix, while solder joints rarely leak, but when they do, the whole system has to be shut down and drained, for the least amount of water in the system will stop the solder sealing the joint.

Taps often drip from around the stem when they are turned on. To stop this, take off the handle. On cross top taps, the handle is held onto the stem by a grub screw, while the retaining screw of a molded handle will be found under the plate at the top that shows hot or cold. Ease this plate off with a screwdriver. Most taps will then have a chrome shield around the stem that has to come off. This shield is screwed onto the base of the tap, and it will take a plumbers' wrench to get it off. The jaws of the wrench can easily damage the chrome so try to pad the jaws with material. When the shield has been removed, you can see the workings of the tap, and a nut, through which the stem passes, can be seen. Turn the tap on, and then very gently tighten that nut, until the leak stops. It will only be a fraction of a turn. Reassemble the top.

If the tap drips from the outlet when fully turned off, the washer needs replacing. Make sure you have a packet of tap washers to hand, and then turn off the water to that tap. Most taps have their own stopcock now, probably under the sink, and then turn the tap on to drain any water in the pipe. Take off the tap handle and the shield (see above). The body of the tap is faced to take a spanner, and so unscrew the body and stem and take off. At the bottom end of the stem there is a washer held in place by a nut. Take this nut off and its washer, replace the old washer with a new one and reassemble the tap. Turn on the water supply. This simple procedure has saved you many pounds.

Houses in Britain are built to last, so our plumbing may go back many years. Some of it may be in Imperial sizes and some metric, and the two will nearly, but not quite, join together. You will need an adaptor to make a join in the two different systems and these are easy to find in a plumbers merchant.

Lead plumbing is still around in many houses, and, provided you do not live in a soft water area, the lead pipes will be coated on the inside with a deposit of calcium that separates the water flow from the lead. This piping is probably quite safe, but it is good practice to replace old lead piping with new materials when doing any renovation work.

Water systems tend to get added to over the years, so when about to begin a plumbing job, turn off the water supply, and then turn on a tap to drain the section of the system you are working on. If you have not in fact isolated the system, the tap will continue to run. This is so much better than undoing the body of a tap, say, and watching it shoot up a column of water. Then what do you do? Try to put the tap back on? Too much pressure. Stop the flow with your thumb? Now how are you going to turn off the supply? Plumbing is much better undertaken with a husband/wife/best friend standing around to help.

There are new plastic fittings for pipes that can just be pushed together. When they came out, they were only used by the plumbingly challenged, formerly known as the clumsy, but now professional plumbers use them all the time.

The water level in a lavatory cistern, or any other water tank, is adjusted by bending the arm of the float ball, but be careful not to bend too far and break it. Do not try to get too much water in a lavatory cistern, because this wastes water every time you flush, and also because water will slowly leak out from the blanking plate on the opposite side from the handle. One of our neighbours over-adjusted this way, and then went off on holiday. By the time they got back water had leaked out, soaked into the plaster ceiling below the lavatory, and the whole lot had come down in the hall.

———

We all have big ideas about the changes we want to make when we move into a new house. Resist the temptation to begin work right away. Live in the house as it is for six months, and you may find the way things are is pretty sensible, and the planned work is not needed at all. Some people who bought a house from us ripped out the adequate if ordinary kitchen, and replaced it with a wonderfully smart and expensive one. The new owner then stood in her transformed room and told us that it had cost more than she had intended, and she did not like it very much. With a little patience, the urge to spend may pass.

Conservatories, even in our cool climate, usually get too hot in the summer, unless they have good shade, but in winter the least sunshine will make them warm, so open the door into the house and get free solar heat.

Few of us are gifted craftsmen, so we need to make up for our deficiencies. One way is to buy the best materials possible, and buy for our own use the best tools we can afford (except paint brushes). Good tools and good materials are nearly always easier to handle and will give better results. A good craftsman can take poor materials and simple tools and create wondrous things, but few of us are that talented.

Building regulations are there to protect us from ourselves, and our neighbours from us. If there is a possibility that the work you are about to undertake could fall within the rules of the building regulations, then phone your local council and ask. The cost of flouting building regulations can be very high.

Man is defined as a tool-using animal. People who say they are no good with machinery, or that they cannot understand computers, are denying a large part of their humanity. The most likely reason is that they are lazy.

An open fire is a picturesque and welcoming feature in any room, but it is about as inefficient a way of heating as can be devised. Most of the heat goes up the chimney. A better heater is a free-standing stove with a glass front. The whole body of the stove takes heat from the fire and radiates it back into the room.

## Carpet basics

If there are small children in your house, consider having a carpet in the kitchen. Carpets are now specially made for kitchens, and they are easy to keep clean. Even if they are relatively expensive, you will make a saving on dishes and glasses, since they have a good chance of surviving being dropped. It is a fact of growth that children will drop plates and glasses, and they are a goner on tiled floors and other hard surfaces.

If a fitted carpet is worn or badly stained in one place, it will be cheaper to buy a good rug to cover the spot than to replace the whole carpet.

Stair carpets become worn on the front edge of the tread, while the vertical piece, the riser, remains almost unworn. Even up the wear by taking up the carpet and shifting it down half a step, so that the riser is now on the step, and the old steps are now risers. It is necessary to cut off the bottom half-step and tack this onto the top riser, but this small loss of neatness is justified by the gain in the life of the carpet.

If there is fresh blood on the carpet – and we will not ask why there is fresh blood on your carpet – it can be removed. Blot up with a cloth and clean, cold, water. If stains remain, try a few drops of hydrogen peroxide left on for a few minutes, and then use a cloth and cold water again.

What can you do with an old carpet? They make good insulation if you have a need, or they can be cut up into squares and used as door mats. When they get dirty, throw them away.

Demolition sites are a grand source of wood, doors, windows and tiles. Ask for the site foreman and strike a deal with him for what you want. Nearly everything on a site will be thrown away, so you are helping to recycle resources by using these materials.

'If it ain't broke, don't fix it' is a good maxim, and it is cheap.

If the urge to modernise your bathtub, sinks and lavatories sweeps over you, resist. Leave the fittings where they are for the next twenty years, and at the end of that time, they will have transformed themselves into highly desirable features. An example would be lavatories with high cisterns and chain pulls. This, of course, does not apply to anything coloured avocado or made of plastic.

Hot grease from cooking poured down the sink cools as it passes through the house drains and out towards the sewer. As it cools, it solidifies, and this lump can become entangled with any small obstruction in the drain. The best way to avoid having to call out someone to clear the drain, is to put all waste cooking fat in an empty container, such as an empty milk carton, and dispose of that in the dustbin.

If your drains get blocked fairly frequently, look for the cause. It is likely to be tree roots growing into the pipe, or the pipe may be broken. It will be cheaper to remove the cause than to treat the symptoms.

If there are long drain runs on your property, then drain rods are a good investment. The cost of the rods will often be less than the cost of a single call-out of a commercial drain-cleaning company. Cleaning drains is not pleasant, but you made the mess. A set of drain rods is an excellent choice of gift for the chap who has everything.

Windows will get broken, so it is worth knowing how to repair them. When replacing a window, get the glass cut 1/8 inch (3mm) smaller than the size of the frame. Clean out all the old putty and put on a coat of primer, then put a small bead of new putty against the back of the frame all the way round to seat the new glass. Push the glass in gently, and then secure it with small nails driven into the frame. Then putty around the outside to make it weather-proof. A kitchen knife makes a good smoothing tool. Leave for a week before painting, but it may be necessary to protect from blue-tits in winter. They love the linseed oil in putty.

If you should find yourself in America, go into a hardware store and ask for a five-in-one. This is a nifty tool that gets the old putty out and the new putty in place.

Here is how to straighten a nail. The want of a nail can hold up a job, so it is worth saving all nails pulled out of old wood. Protect your eyes. Put the bent nail on a hard surface, such as the back of a vice, and hold down the point with the left hand. With the bend up, tap the nail with a light hammer, striking only the nail, and not the left hand. A very badly bent nail can sometimes be straightened by first squeezing in a vice, and then proceeding as above.

You might as well save any screws you take out, provided the shoulders of the slot in the head have not been smoothed over. If they are damaged, it is better to throw the screw away.

Before throwing away a useless piece of equipment, try to disassemble it and recover nuts and bolts, and screws. Thread the nuts and bolts together before storing in a box. A wide selection of nuts, bolts, washers, and screws will always come in useful.

Reclaimed timber is often of better quality than new timber. The place to find a supplier of reclaimed timber is in the Yellow Pages, and if you go to the yard you will find timber that has been salvaged from offices, churches, and old houses. There will be everything from floorboards to rafters. Pick up a piece and note the weight. Most of it is much heavier, i.e., denser, than new wood. It will be dirty, and will probably have nails in it, but, size for size, it can be half the price of new, and a lot stronger. If you have any suspicions that there may be rot in the wood, then treat with a proprietary wood preserver.

Sometimes it becomes necessary to lift a floor board to get at a pipe joint or an electrical junction box. Do not nail the board back, but fix it down with screws, so that the next time it will be much easier to get it up again.

If you live in a town and want to keep livestock, then keep bees. They do better in town than in the country, because it is a little bit warmer in towns, and all the flower gardens give them a long season for gathering nectar. Half of England is convinced that they will die if stung by a bee. This is nonsense, or our ancestors would have all been killed off when bees were kept as the only source of sweetness. On the other hand, it is not a bad story to put about, for it may keep vandals out of your garden.

Thick curtains are an added layer of insulation and that helps to save heat. Thick curtains also protect alcohol-crazed eyeballs from direct sunlight.

## Furniture for less than a fortune

Lots of modern furniture, with its straight lines, is easy to make. Go along to your favourite store and choose a design you like, take out your measuring tape, measure it up, write down the sizes, and then go home and make it.

Buying old, good furniture, and then cleaning, stripping, repairing and polishing will give you a houseful of furniture that will be a credit to you, while spending twice the sum on new furniture will still give you something pretty ordinary.

Re-upholstering furniture can save you an awful lot of money, but you really need to know what you are doing, so take a class first. We've done quite a bit of simple re-doing, but finally had a go at an upholstered chair, without the benefit of a class. Being of practical natures, we took photographs as we disemboweled it, so that we could see exactly how it would go back together. Finally, as it stood in the middle of the room, a bare wooden frame of little resemblance to the fat comfortable seat of the week before, the film was eagerly awaited. Alas, the film had never 'caught' on the spool of the old second-hand camera, and we spent a small fortune on the phone to our friend who had done the class.

Decent wood furniture is made strong by well-made joints – mortise and tenon, dovetail, by the use of dowels, and so on. Furniture tends to fall apart at the joints because the glue has gone after many years, and a good repair will involve taking the joint completely apart, cleaning out the old glue, and re-glue-ing with modern furniture glue. There is no point trying to force glue into an assembled joint; it will not work.

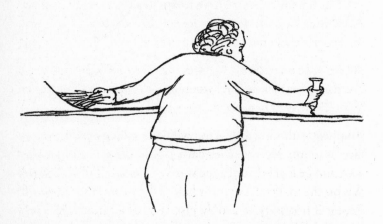

When doing any repair, on furniture or anything else, try to really do a good one. It is often possible to botch up a repair, so that it will hold for a while, but then it will fail again. Be bold. Take the whole thing apart, go further than necessary, go for it.

This is when you discover the real problem, the one that is causing the symptoms.

If a repair to a piece of furniture requires, say, a piece of oak, it is often cheaper to go to a sale and buy an old and ugly oak wardrobe and knock it apart to get the piece you want, than to buy the oak from a timber merchant.

Stripping off old paint is easy and inexpensive. Provided the furniture surface is flat, the best method of all is simply to use a scraping tool, sandpaper and elbow grease. No chemicals. No napalm.

One of the best tools for dealing with intricate furniture is a sandpaper sponge.

Stripping paint from a wood door is a big job, but lots of doors need stripping, so people have set up businesses to do it. It gets dipped into a tank of really powerful stripper and will come out quite clean, and it is not expensive.

White rings on polished surfaces can be removed by rubbing it out using a very fine steel wool (grade 0000) and linseed oil. Wipe clean and then polish.

Another method of removing white rings from polished surfaces is to mix together four parts olive oil to one part paraffin wax, and heat gently until the wax has melted. When cool, rub this on the marks, leave it for half an hour, and then wipe off. Repeat if necessary. It is only just short of a miracle. We keep a jar of this in the cleaning box.

If a piece of furniture is seriously dirty, then polishing will only cover over the dirt. The best furniture cleaner ever, and worth trying before you start to refinish a piece, is: two parts vinegar, three parts pure turpentine, three parts boiled linseed oil. You buy boiled linseed oil. Now add a small amount of elbow grease, a couple of old rags and you may need do nothing else to that grotty old chest of drawers or cupboard.

Did you know that woodworm only enters furniture at unpolished surfaces? Therefore, once a year it would be wise to polish the whole piece with beeswax-turpentine polish.

To make beeswax polish. Three times as much PURE TURPENTINE as pure clean beeswax (i.e. 100g beeswax, 300ml turpentine). Gently melt the beeswax – remember it is flammable – and stir in the turpentine. Pour into a jar or plastic screwtop container, leave to cool before putting on the lid. You can adjust proportions to suit – if you want a thinner polish, add more turpentine, or for a hard wax polish use more beeswax. It really works on furniture, metal or leather. Don't forget there is one other ingredient you must add: elbow grease. On the other hand, you really need only apply this once a year – just dust off in the interim.

A scratch in furniture can be filled in with beeswax. If the furniture is dark, you can rub it first with one of the oily nuts, such as walnut, pecan or a Brazil nut to restore much of the colour.

———

Repointing brickwork is tedious, but well within the ability range of any householder. It takes time, and is therefore expensive, if done by a contractor. Repointing is needed when the cement between the bricks has flaked away, leaving deep undercutting of the bricks. This undercutting allows rain to penetrate into the wall, and frost will start to break up the bricks. The old, powdery cement between the bricks has to be removed until firm cement is reached. This loose cement can be raked or brushed out, either with a special chisel or with some tool that fits the gap between the bricks. Ready-mix cement for repointing can be bought from a builders merchant, or you can mix your own using three parts builders sand to one part cement, and then mix to a stiff texture. When you have made a complete mix, draw the point of a trowel across the mix. The point should slide through easily, but the sides of the cut should stay sharp and clean. That is a good mix. In the North, the mortar is trowelled into the gap between the bricks to make bricks and mortar flush, but in the South the mortar is cut back from under the top brick to present a slope to the rain and weather. I think this looks better. Repointing is a job that can be done a little at a time, until all the damage is repaired.

Christmas trees are usually thrown away or burnt in January, but if the tree has a straight trunk it can be used as a post or plant support in the garden, once stripped of its branches.

Flat roofs are cheap to build, but they always leak, and the place where the rain is getting in is hard to find. You know where it is coming in on the inside, but that can be yards from where the rain is penetrating the tar on the outside, so the whole thing becomes an expensive mess. Therefore, never build, or have built for you, a flat roof. Even a shallow slope on a roof will help. Save yourself lots of expense and frustration, and just say 'No' to flat roofs.

When wiring a light switch, always run the live wire to the switch, not the neutral. The switch will work, either way, but if the neutral goes to the switch, that leaves the live wire going to the socket when the light is switched off, and it is not safe practice, and I wish they would stop it. If anyone wants a pair of pliers with little round bits burnt out of the cutting edge caused by cutting live wires, I have a supply.

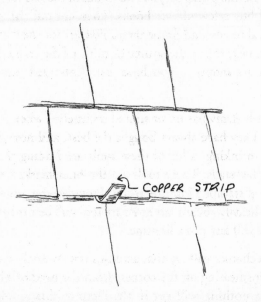

A roof slate that has come loose can be fastened back by getting a thin strip of copper about 1 inch (25mm) wide that is about the length of the slate, and drill a hole in one end for the nail. Pull the old slate completely out, and, if it is not broken, it can be used again. Underneath, you will see that the removed slate covered the two edges of the slates below. Slide a hacksaw blade down between those two slates, and you will locate a wooden batten to which they are nailed. Now nail your copper strip to that batten, between the slates. Slide the loose tile back into position and bend up the end of the copper strip to hold the tile in place.

Where are you going to find copper strips? Hot water tanks are made of copper sheet, and they are always getting replaced. Keep your eyes open.

If you want fine prints on your walls, haunt second-hand book sales and buy a few old art books. Then cut out the pictures that appeal to you and frame them. Fine art for the cost of the frame. In fact, this is the source of most of the framed prints found in art shops, so you have just eliminated the middle man.

The British Army has never stinted themselves when it comes to tools. They have always bought the best, and now that the Army is shrinking, a lot of these tools are finding their way onto market stalls. These tools are the ones marked with an arrow head stamped into the metal. Provided the tool has not been too heavily abused, an ex-Army tool will be the best of its type, and will last you a lifetime.

Many mechanics will say that an adjustable wrench is a clever device for smearing off the corners from the head of a bolt, so that then nothing will get it off. Despite this opinion, an adjustable wrench does allow you to move most bolts, without having to buy a whole set of spanners, Imperial and metric.

## The paper with a thousand uses

You can make furniture from newspaper, as in papier-mâché! But you have to be terribly clever. Much easier, though, are placemats. Roll sheets of newspaper really tightly and tie with string, looping the rolls very closely together to make something not unlike grass mats. If you use coloured magazine pages and roll them diagonally, you will get cheerful patterns.

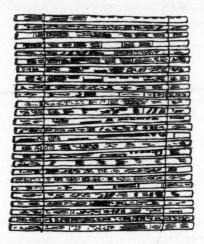

Make your own conservatory blinds by rolling newspaper tightly and tying off, just like the placemats, but wider and longer. The 'grass mat' effect will let light dapple into the conservatory. Penny pinching? Approximate saving: £990.

A hot summer day? Pleat a newspaper to make a fan.

Papier-mâché is made of finely chopped up paper and white glue. It is a wonderful, sticky, tactile stuff, and you can make puppets, dolls, and all sorts of small, useful things.

Maps, newspapers, cartoons – all can be used in place of wallpaper. It is only one step away from covering walls with posters, after all.

You can make a fun lampshade with newspaper. Blow up a balloon and smear it with vaseline and cover it with papier-mâché while still wet with white glue. Leave until hard, then poke the balloon with a pin, and there is a lampshade. Unless the balloon was very large, it is best to use a low-watt bulb.

The better sort of tramp spreads newspapers on a bench before lying down, to keep insulated from draughts. He will also slip newspapers under a jacket to make it wind-proof.

———————

When you are decorating and want to get rid of old decals that children always seem to have stuck on their windows, soak them off with a little vinegar.

Always have a supply of scruffy clothes ready to put on at a moment's notice. Otherwise, when an interesting job involving bends in a soil pipe, or something leaking from under the car, has to be done, either you give up because it would ruin good clothes, or, more likely, you do the job, hoping to remain clean, and your hopes are dashed, yet again.

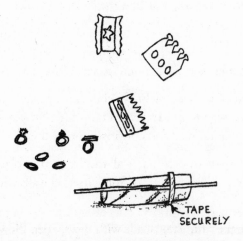

Once you have made your own Christmas crackers you will probably never want another commercial one. About the only thing you will need to buy are the snappers themselves, and they cost only pennies from art and craft shops, and tiny toys if you wish. Everything else can be made, or recycled, or you will already have lurking in cupboards. Put all the little goodies, rings, puzzles and treasures onto the silly hat, roll them up or put them in paper bags, and slide them into the cardboard tube from a loo roll. Tape on the snapper, then put on the outside paper and trimmings.

Things made of plastic are notorious for little, vital, bits breaking off, and glues do not always work with plastic. If you have an electric solder iron the tip can be used to melt the plastic and fuse the parts back together.

Even old election posters have their uses. The better sort of candidates have ones made out of plastic and printed both sides, and these can be cleaned down and used on a work bench for assembly work requiring freedom from fluff and grit, say when putting a carburettor back together.

Before spending loads of money on redecorating your home, it is a good idea to visit a few friends, and try to see their houses as though they were your own. Observe the cracks in the ceiling. Note the threadbare carpet. Their homes too have chipped paint and shabby corners that you had never observed before, because we are much harder on ourselves than we are on others. Now look at your home again. Do you really have to redecorate?

For a really belligerent screw that just refuses to come out, first set a screwdriver in the slot and then hit the handle of the screwdriver with a hammer. This often frees up the screw and it can be taken out in the usual way. If that screw still puts up resistance, then get out your brace and put in a special screwdriver bit, and with that you can apply terrific power – so much so that it is easy to tear the head right off the screw. Then you have got a real problem.

'Neither a borrower nor a lender be' is a sour-faced philosophy. It speaks of a dim-witted suspicion of your fellow man, which, for the most part, is unjustified. It often makes more sense to ask a neighbour if you can borrow his special tool, a hub-puller, say, than buy one yourself. It is polite to return a tool on time, and if you try to return it in better condition than when you borrowed it, you will find that people will lend to you again. And you must be willing to lend your tools, too.

DIY work pays. Example: for rebuilding the roof on a single garage, builders quote £400. DIY job using best materials, £140. Example: neighbours' gate to back garden, done by local builder, £420. Mine to serve the same purpose and at least as effective, £23.

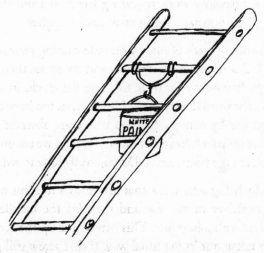

There are enough problems when working on a ladder without having to worry about the paint tin falling off. An answer is to take an old wire coat hanger – for an extra-strong job, tape two hangers together – and squeeze the two arms together. Now bend these arms down about four inches (10cm) from each end to make hooks to go over the rungs of the ladder. The paint tin hangs from the hook that went over the clothes rail. I have fallen off a ladder, but I have never lost a drop of paint.

We, the plodding foot soldiers of the DIY army, are pretty slow, and when we stop to work out how much we are saving for every hour of work we put in, the answer is usually not very much. We may only be saving £1 an hour through our efforts, but, if we would not be earning anything in that hour anyway, then we are £1 better off. That is more than you will earn watching TV.

# 5

# Recycling to Save Money and Maybe the Planet

*Something from nothing is a lot more rewarding than something that cost the earth and is still worth nothing.*

We have read that the whole recycling craze started over beer cans on the Continent. One country was trying to prevent another country getting into their market, so banned the foreign product on the grounds that the cans weren't recyclable.

You could be forgiven for thinking that the very *word* recycling has been changed by bureaucracy – it used to mean that we re-used something in a new way – now it refers to hauling waste material at great cost to us all to be separated out, chopped up, melted, and added back into manufacturing processes so that councils can meet their targets for stopping global warming, and consumers can feel a warm glow because they have 'recycled' unnecessary packaging. But consumers haven't recycled at all, they have simply thrown out something after just one use.

So when we talk about recycling, we mean re-using something yourself, several times over if possible. If you buy a carton of yogurt, eat the yogurt and put the carton into the recycling bin, that's a single use by you – if you re-use the carton for storing food in the freezer, then perhaps use it for storing something else and finally use it as a plant pot, that is recycling!

By all means use the recycle bins, the orange bags, the blue boxes, the black boxes, the green wheelie bins – after all the only person that can make any real difference in recycling is YOU – and it all helps, we hope.

What CAN you do with an empty tin can? Here's another 30 Uses list from *The Penny Pincher Paper* – of course, you always get 31 uses in these.

1. Use for repairing car exhausts – tomato puree tins are just about the right size.
2. Tins are just right for cleaning paint brushes.
3. Flatten, pop rivet in for car body repairs, then cover with filler.

4. Tins of all shapes and sizes make excellent pencil holders, decorated or not.

5. Boston Brown Bread is always steamed in tin cans, especially ones with many ridges.

6. Two tin cans and a long string doth a toy telephone make.

7. Cut stars and shapes in the side of a tin and use for a candle holder.

8. Use as a unit of measure. Just the right size can be found for most things.

9. Soldiers bury an empty tin in the ground, fill it with petrol and light it. Then cook on top. Air cannot get in at the sides, so it burns slowly.

10. Hang tins on string so that they bang together in the wind as a bird scarer.

11. Put all the unfiled bills and invoices in a tin until you can get around to them.

12. Fill with water and put a wet paint brush in it. It will stop an oil-based paint from drying out for days. Just take out again, shake off any water, and go back to painting.

13. Use a tin can to mix up poster paints and hand over to the children.

14. Use as a small reservoir of material for any coating like Waxoyl or creosote. These come in gallon-plus tins with a small opening, and have to be decanted before use. There are lots of things that come in tins like that.

15. Keep your jewellery in a boring empty tin in the larder. Thieves don't have time to look there.

16. Empty tin cans make excellent scoops.

17. Use to catch oil drips under your car.

18. Squeeze the top of the tin to make a pouring spout. Now this can be used for jobs such as getting petrol from a large container, like a jerry can, into the lawn mower.

19. Use for collections of nuts, bolts, nails, etc.

20. Cut down the side and flatten. Then nail over the top of fence posts to stop water, and hence rots, damaging the posts.

21. Use as candle moulds.

22. Use to hold the egg for poached eggs.

23. When separating out beeswax from honey that has set solid, put the whole comb, in bits, into a tin, then heat that in a pan of water. The wax comes to the top and can be taken off when cool.

24. If you have a large tin, say 1-gallon size, take out top and bottom, punch holes in the sides, set in the barbecue, put paper in the bottom and charcoal on top, and light the paper. When the coals are hot, carefully take off the tin and spread out the coals.

25. Use as a posting container for things that *really* need protection.

26. Fill with creosote. Then put the end of fence posts that are going into the ground into the tins and let them soak for several days.

27. Take large tins, say paint tins, paint them a cheerful colour and use as planters on a patio.

28. Put a little jam and water in a tin, cover the top with paper held by a rubber band, punch holes in the paper and set out as a wasp trap.

29. If the light from your inspection lamp gets in your eyes, as mine does, make a reflector out of a flattened coffee tin.

30. Put a firecracker under a tin. It makes a loud noise and sends the tin flying into the air. For the totally irresponsible.
31. Use as target practice, if you have a six-shooter. It looks easy enough in the Westerns!


Everybody knows about slicing rubber gloves into 'rubber bands' – wonder how many people actually do it?

Vegetable peelings go first into the stockpot. Then onto the compost heap.

Plastic net bags that hold oranges and lemons make good scourers for anything that needs nylon scouring.

An old flush door put across two chests of drawers makes a sewing or work table.

When the plastic milk bottle is empty and clean, cut off the bottom corner at an angle to make a super scoop. Or cut the bottle in half and use the bottom as a mini-dustbin and the top as a funnel.

Use carrier bags as wastepaper bin liners, but if you use them in the kitchen waste bin, make sure they're fairly free from holes and slits in the bottom.

Envelopes are perfect for filing anything and everything, especially the large ones with windows so that you can see what's inside. Used envelopes work just as well as new ones, and a cardboard box makes a good file cabinet. Use what you have!

While you can't re-use rubber jar rings for preserving, they can be put aside for other uses around the house, such as sewing them to bottoms of slippy rugs.

Map out of date? Turn it into a lampshade.

Save fabric remnants for quilts or mending, making children's clothes or craft projects.

A piece of velvet makes a good record cleaner, for those of us who are old-fashioned enough to have a piece of velvet and records.

A piece of velvet or corduroy makes an excellent press cloth for pile fabrics, and isn't so painful as a needleboard.

Save yarn scraps, which can be knitted up into squares for blankets or for embroidery and tapestry or dolls' hair.

Zips are like buttons. Save them. Keep them organised. Use them again.

Transparent lipstick cases, cleaned out thoroughly, make a tiny housewife in purse or suit pocket or a container for sets of buttons.

Quilt interlining scraps can be used to make soft house shoes, using either sweatshirt or denim for the outside of the shoe.

Keep ribbon neatly furled around a cardboard roll, and pinned down with a straight pin. You always need ribbon.

Gift wrap is better kept furled *inside* its cardboard tube, each end closed with a recycled lid from other packaging to keep the wrap clean.

Cut apart an outdated dress and make it into an apron.

Sheets can be cut down for curtain lining. Curtain lining can be cut down for cot sheets. Cot sheets can be cut down for pillowcases. Pillowcases can be cut down for handkerchiefs. Handkerchiefs can be cut down for bandages. Bandages can be cut down for dustcloths. Dustcloths can be cut down for potpourri sachets. Pot-pourri sachets can be cut down for stuffing toys.

It is bordering on waste if you don't pass baby clothes and equipment around the family and friends.

If things are saved, they should be kept tidy and organised! It's no use hoarding something for seven years if, when it's just what you need, you can't find it and have to buy a replacement anyway. You KNOW you'll find the stashed one three days later.

Save any bit or piece of dowelling! Large for planting beans, small for homemade quilting frame, dolls' house or toy garage.

Save magazines! Or burn them. Or cut them apart and file the bits of information you want. Or pass them on to someone else to read.

Save string. You can never have enough string.

Your own hair can be recycled. Either put it out for the birds to use in their nests or put it onto the compost heap, but don't throw it away.

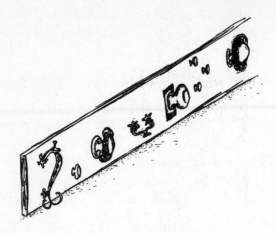

Door knobs, drawer knobs, bed knobs. Save them all and mount them on a board on the wall, and you have a coat rack.

Firelighters: Newspaper. Waxed cartons from milk or juice. Candle ends. Anything soaked in a LITTLE paraffin. Dried orange, lemon or grapefruit peels. Empty cardboard tubes or envelopes packed with paper or twigs. Used wine corks.

Tightly-closing tins such as large instant coffee ones, golden syrup and small baking powder ones, make good toys for small children.

Bits and pieces of odd and broken jewellery are always useful – perhaps for the dolls' house, or for the dressing-up box.

Recycle crayons – melt down in dariole moulds, mince pie tins or foil dishes in a warm oven while something else is baking.

Real keys on a real key ring – children love them. Not your current car ones.

Offcuts of card can be a real problem for packaging companies and printers, but they may be free for asking, and are great for crafts and drawing.

Screw-top glacé cherry containers keep an 18-month-old quiet for four days. Also good for storing small toys.

Have a toy circle in your circle of friends and neighbours.

Save quizzes or riddles from papers and magazines and store them for using in Christmas crackers.

A perfect toy box: the sectioned wooden bulb boxes from garden centres and greengrocers'. If you have a tame greengrocer, ask him for one.

Orange boxes from your friendly greengrocer can be transformed with a Stanley knife into dolls' house furniture.

Beautiful dolls' house linens are made from old shirts and blouses.

You could be swamped by gift tags cut from just one year's Christmas cards. But you can make bookmarks, postcards, little gift boxes, recipe file cards, spools for spare threads or ribbons, backings for photographs in a frame, bases for doing needlepoint lace, miniature 'box kites' for tree decorations, quilt pattern pieces, message pads or blocks, pompom bases, toddlers' books by sewing several together, collage pictures, a carpet-protector when painting the skirting board, stencil patterns, a crumb-scoop for the table, paper chains, Advent calendars, postcards for thank-you's or New Year cards, jigsaw puzzles … and finally they can warm you twice – once when you receive them, and again when you burn them.

Egg white makes an excellent glue for paper. It is not an economical glue for paper, though, if you break an egg just for the stickiness and then waste the rest of the egg.

For fast dusting, or brass polishing, slip an old pair of socks over your hands. Rubber gloves dissolve in brass polish anyway.

Old sock tops on the wrists keep water from dripping down your arms when you're reaching up cleaning.

And cotton socks, bless them, are excellent cleaning cloths.

'They say everything in the world is good for something' – Dryden. Even a discarded banana skin. The inside of the skin will clean patent leather shoes, and if you happen to own a donkey as well, you've made his day, it's one of his favourite snacks!

Tights or stockings make good strainers. They can also be cut into long spirals to make twine.

Towels which are past their best and about to join the cleaning/dust cloth pile are a bit big. Usually, though, there are only two areas that are badly decomposing, and with a nifty pair of scissors you can make several small washcloths, which are absolutely WONDERFUL for babies and small children – you need dozens of these (washcloths, not children).

Plastic bottles make excellent moulds for candles, whether you are making new or recycled ones.

An old saying is that patchwork quilts warm you in more ways than one – once when you're scrabbling among the fabric scraps to find the right colour, again when you're stitching it all together and it envelops you, the table and the sewing machine, once more when you sleep under it and finally when you look at it and remember the dress made for a child who is grown-up.

Beautiful wool can be found in out-of-fashion sweaters, at charity shops and jumble sales. With a little bit of ingenuity and a lot of patience, you can unravel the wool, wind it into skeins, handwash and let dry, then wind into balls for re-knitting.

Tall, thin bottles make good rolling pins (it's all my mother ever used!).

Sell clutter. William Morris: 'Have nothing in your houses that you do not know to be useful or believe to be beautiful.'

Use two jars for white spirit – one in which the brushes are first dunked, and when the sediment has settled, pour the clean spirit off into another jar which is for the next stage of cleaning. When the sediment has hardened in the jar, scrape it out and put in the base of a bonfire.

You can even recycle used engine oil. Keep a little for wiping over tools before you put them away – but DON'T keep oily cloths crumpled up in a corner, they can go up in flames if they get too warm. The rest of used engine oil should go to the municipal dump – there is NO EXCUSE WHATSOEVER for pouring used oil down a drain or in the street.

Save a few wine corks – stick them on the end of knitting needles to keep the stitches from sliding off the end, and they also make a nonscratch scourer as well as being good firelighters.

If you learn nothing else from this book learn this: if you have children, do not deprive them of the greatest plaything known to mankind – the dressing-up box. Throw all your outdated evening dresses and strippy-strappy heels, your cricket sweater and school jacket into this, add ingredients for a magic show and the children will find the real things a thousand times more fun than plastic toys. The box itself can be something recycled ... our childhood one was a coffin case!

Those curtains about to be discarded could be super teatowels or dishcloths.

Before you throw away an old chest of drawers, make sure that the handles or knobs aren't worth more than the chest! They could probably be used on a different chest, at least – and the wood can be recycled several times.

Shredded newspaper can be used instead of or with straw or wood shavings for stabling a horse. There is an added advantage that horses will not eat it.

Veterinary surgeries are usually grateful for your newspapers.

Save all candle ends to melt down and make new candles, using plastic bottles, tins, and such for moulds. However, you will have to buy new wick! Our first effort many years ago was a disappointment – the candles simply would not light! When we went back to the shop where we had bought the string we used, the shopkeeper explained that she wasn't surprised they wouldn't burn, as the string was meant for hanging pictures and was fireproof.

As coat hangers obviously breed and multiply in the wardrobe, new uses must constantly be found for them. In addition to sticking them into the car radio aerial hole, they're just right for barbecue skewers and for bending into a frame for holding clothespeg bags you've made – perhaps from old curtains.

Wood-burning stoves will burn almost anything that is burnable. They burn newspapers rather well, so if no other use can be found for your old papers, burn them in addition to wood or instead of wood. After all, paper is just processed tree.

Almost everyone who writes to us at the *The Penny Pincher Paper* sends their letter in a re-used envelope.

Making your own paper is both fun and inexpensive. You need a kit, or the materials and ability to make a filtering screen, but after that there is no special equipment needed, just lots of scrap paper, newspaper and, for really special quality paper, some old rags. Notice on very good stationery the phrase 'high rag content'.

And here's how to use up slivers of soap: Collect enough slivers to equal about a bar of soap, you want them rather dry. Scrape away and discard any unsightly grey bits. Shred the slivers into any plastic container such as shaped bubble packaging, soap mould or similar pretty shape (sea shells work, too). Fill the mould to the brim, pack down, refill right up to the top, and then gently pour in warm water to the top. Leave to dry –

several days – smoothing down the top from time to time. When completely dry, tip out and let dry hard. If you always buy different colours of soap you will have lovely marbled bars, which won't fall apart.

Not only are egg boxes just right for storing fragile Christmas ornaments, you can also MAKE ornaments from some kinds.

A non-damaging doorstop: a thick (old) sponge, simply jamming it between the door and the floor or the door and the frame.

Soap-chipping or string-saving won't make you rich, but doing so helps you think before throwing something away. It also saves a little bit of soap and a little bit of string.

Christmas tree decorations are not one of the essentials of life, so we spend very little on them. On the other hand, we never throw away any of our decorations, and we take off and store the tinsel for the next year – and the year after that. The result of years of accumulation is that our tree is usually described as 'gross'. The angel has been on the top of every tree since 1963.

And that string?

30 Uses for Pieces of String too Short to Use

1. Put them out for the birds to use in their nests.
2. Add to the compost heap.
3. Use when making your own paper (rag content, you see).
4. Give to the play group to make string pictures.
5. Knot together to make longer pieces of string.
6. Push into gaps in floorboards or window frames or into holes in plaster walls.
7. Use in toy or pillow stuffing.

8. Glue onto greetings cards for decorations.
9. Renovate Christmas decorations by gluing pieces of string onto old ornaments and painting gold or silver.
10. Coil into circles, stitch circles together for drinks coasters.
11. Make a pompom with odds and ends of string for the kitten.
12. Use pieces of string for a rag doll's hair.
13. Hang wooden spoons or ornaments by drilling a hole in the end, and making a loop of string for hanging.
14. Use as a key ring, making a jolly good knot.
15. With a great deal of patience, you could make a net shopping bag.
16. Make 'tufts' on soft pillows for chairs, by tying short pieces in a pattern over the pillow.
17. You need only a short piece of string for 'Pin the Tail on the Donkey'.
18. Use as wicks for short candles. First, make sure it isn't fireproof string.
19. A loop of string will last a few minutes as an emergency zip pull.
20. Tie in a loop of string at the waist of repaired tights to make finding them easier.
21. Make hanging loops for skirts.
22. A substitute for a ring binder are string loops through the holes in the pages.
23. A very short piece of string can be tied around the junctions of strings wrapped around parcels for sending in the post, making a very secure package.
24. There is a weird and wonderful counting device, called a *quipu,* used by the ancient Peruvians to keep accounts, which is pieces of string of varying lengths, with knots.

25. Short pieces of string can be included in rag rugs to give texture and colour.
26. By tying knots over and over in a short piece of string, it should end up as a ball suitable for use as a button.
27. Another type of string button can be made by making a small ball of string and then working buttonhole stitch around and around it.
28. A unique chatelaine could be made with various pieces of string [that is, a collection of household things such as thimble, keys, scissors, hung on cords, then suspended from the waist].
29. A decorative tassel could be made with odds and ends of string, particularly of coloured strings say to be used as a pull on a light cord.
30. A short piece of string will make a loop for buttons.
31. All the best spy stories have the hero slipping a short piece of string into the leaves of his book, so that when he returns he can tell whether his room has been searched.

# 6

# Gardening and Healthy Eating

All things come to he who waiteth ... as long as he worketh like heck while he waiteth.

While our three children were growing up, we lived in rural Cheshire, surrounded by six acres where we kept the usual pony, donkey, geese, chickens, and French exchange students, and where we decided that self-indulgency was a lot more fun than self-sufficiency – it's just as easy to grow asparagus and globe artichokes as lettuce and potatoes.

Even if you don't like gardening when you start doing it, you'll come to love it.

As soon as wood ashes are cool, scoop them up and put them straight onto the garden. Soft fruit especially benefits.

Egg cartons make good 'peat pots' for starting plants.

If you're lucky enough to find wool-nylon mix yarn, especially in green, it makes fantastic death-defying garden twine.

Plan ahead on your vegetable planting. Little and often with lettuces – gluts are hard to deal with. Choose varieties of vegetables to suit your family. If they hate broad beans perhaps they'll like French beans better.

Plant vegetables that will fill the 'Hungry Gap' in early spring when perennials such as artichokes and asparagus have completely disappeared and it is unlikely that there will be beans and lettuces around. Broccoli, cabbage, celery, chicory, corn salad, dandelion, Jerusalem artichoke, leeks, parsnips, spring greens and swede will keep starvation at bay. We have a list of twenty-five vegetables you can grow in your own back garden to be harvested in the Hungry Gap – and people eat frozen peas and beans all winter??

An Epicurean, free, vegetable also in the Hungry Gap: if you have Brussels sprouts in the garden, let the last few 'sprout' to about four or five inches long, steam them and they are very like asparagus.

Plant rhubarb.

Mulching works! Bolted lettuces make an excellent mulch along bean plants. If you don't cover bare earth, God will, and He uses a lot of weeds.

The best bird-scarer is free, bio-degradable and very, very quiet. First, obtain a dead bird. Attach one leg to a branch with a piece of string, letting the wings and head hang down to flap gently in the breeze.

Next best bird-scarer is tape – such as cassette or old computer tape – wound around in a tree, or stretched between two sticks along a row – twisted as it's wound so that it pulsates with light reflections.

Jam jars or larger jars turned upside down over delicate plants make a mini greenhouse. Even plastic bottles can be cut in half and shoved in the ground to give plants a chance to grow before the slugs and snails pig the lot.

Do you grow broad beans? Do you let blackfly enjoy YOUR feast of beantops?

Corn-salad or lamb's lettuce is pretty, and thrives in the Hungry Gap. Let it develop its seed heads which add delicious crunch to early salads. It re-seeds prolifically but is easy to yoick out.

Use sand, not salt, on icy paths – salt can damage or even kill nearby plants, the sand can be swept up and used again and again.

Cut off a lettuce instead of pulling out the root, and it will grow another, smaller, looser lettuce.

For early salads, mix together leftover edible-leaf vegetable seeds such as lettuce, beetroot, spinach, parsley and other herbs, and plant in a row or block for cutting salad, or for pulling up what is wanted and letting, say, all the spinach that remains grow on to maturity.

Yogurt or cream cartons make super potting-up pots for young plants. Poke holes in the bottom with a skewer. You probably have enough sense to avoid your hand and fingers.

If you're cold in the garden, you aren't gardening hard enough.

Moles don't like noise. Any kind of noise – stamping, hitting the ground with a shovel, wind blowing across the necks of bottles inserted into their runs.

Invest in a water butt if you don't have one. Your plants don't need processed water.

Find work and gardening clothes at jumble sales. Ten pence for a sweater means less agony if you shred it than if you shred your Guernsey.

Cold tea really, really does make a good plant food – indoors or out – and tea leaves make excellent food for roses. Coffee grounds are fine for sprinkling around, too.

Plan your garden to be a gourmet one. It's a waste of space to grow something that's dirt cheap in the shops and do without asparagus, artichokes, radicchio and chicory.

Swap plant cuttings with friends. Swap. Not swipe.

Stretch the feet of tights or stockings around a circle of strong wire such as clothes hanger. Secure with string and attach to a long pole for a handy fruit-picker, or a device for skimming off pond weed. Though don't forget that pond weed is actually an oxygenating plant. You may not like it, but the fish do.

Store bulbs in tights or stockings.

Old tights and stockings can be used for tying plants to stakes so that they are not strangled.

If you make hanging baskets, rake or scrape moss from your lawn or path … there always seems to be at least one damp, dank corner of a garden that nurtures moss.

Eggshells can be crushed and added to the compost heap, or steeped in water to make a liquid feed for lime-loving plants, or just added to acid soils.

Save your own seeds to supplement those that you buy. Remember that $F_1$ seeds won't come true, so skip those except for curiosity's sake.

Every year in the kitchen garden some crops will do really well but others fail. And every year it will be different crops.

Cats don't like black pepper. Rotten onions work, too, and these can be got free from a greengrocer. Of course it might keep YOU out of the garden as well!

There are only two sorts of plant: the quick and the dead. If a plant is malingering, it is a waste of space.

Inside or outside, half a plastic bottle makes a superb cloche for plants – just don't try to fool yourself into thinking it's a Victorian bell cloche, it's half a plastic bottle.

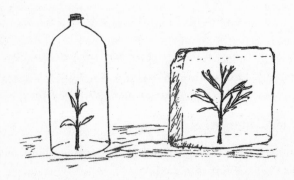

The garden is a *sanctum sanctorum*, the place to go instead of spending money on entertainment. All the world is in the garden.

Washing-up water can be used on plants.

Avoid chemical weedkillers and pesticides like the plague. Not only are they potential people killers, they are exceedingly unkind to your wallet. If a packet of seeds only cost 50p, why pay £4.50 to try to save them from aphids? A little soap or detergent diluted in a spray bottle works if you can't bear to pull up the plant.

If you have carrot fly in your garden, don't try to grow carrots. Buy carrots from the greengrocer and grow something else in your garden.

A large old table fork from jumble sale, antique stall, car boot or charity shop is a wonderful weeder, planter, and transplanting tool.

Globe artichokes are delicious and if you grow them yourself, they are free. Even better, they multiply, and their progeny are just as delicious. The plants are attractive, can even be grown alongside flowers, suppress weeds underneath them, and are diabolically difficult to dig up when their useful life is over, but it's worth it!

Another gourmet crop to grow oneself if there is possibly room is sweetcorn. The old saying is that you can walk to the garden to cut sweetcorn but you must run back to the kitchen to cook it, and if you ever taste really fresh corn you will know it's true. This is the crop besides swede that really is greedy about the room it takes, though, because you must plant it in a block, not rows.

Soft fruit, and indeed tree fruit, will save you hundreds of pounds over just a very few years. Grow your favourites, and consider yourself lucky if you have pears, cherries and quinces in your garden.

Even the smallest garden ought to have a few asparagus plants, just for luxury and the beauty of the ferns in flower arrangements.

One of the joys in gardening is the perversity of it all! The gardening books will agree that some plant or other will thrive only in sand, full sun, fed with potash on the third Thursday of November etc etc – yet every so often our experience has been that a delicate little specimen such as bay has been crammed into the windiest scrawniest piece of clay, prayed over briefly and left to grow into an eight-foot beauty. There's no reason.

Horseradish will take over the world.

So will mint.

Perpetual spinach is a must. Grow a few plants of summer spinach to see things bolt, but perpetual spinach is a year-round delight.

Marrow is another crop that varies according to when you harvest it – small courgettes, satisfying marrows, and if you can bear to forgo some of the fruit, the flowers can be cooked in batter, but this is rather like eating baby corncobs – why not wait until it grows up and gives you more?

And there are always one or two courgettes that hide underneath leaves and make you jump when you find the two-foot monsters. Get them out quick as they diminish the crop coming on. Make chutney.

Turnips are a bit like sweetcorn – unless you've had them straight from the garden, you've been eating them à la Scarlett O'Hara – pithy and dry. The greens are delicious!

Keep at least one grape vine if just for its leaves. Greek dolmades, homemade, is one of the great dishes of the world, and very economical to make.

Ground elder was originally planted as a garden vegetable. Eating it is such sweet revenge.

Plan your gardening so that you have small amounts of many different vegetables coming on all the time – use your freezer for storing gluts of fruits, which freeze better than you can freeze your own vegetables, and are more expensive in the shops.

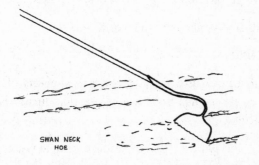

SWAN NECK
HOE

It's all a matter of preference, but years of experience have shown that the vegetables sheared off by a Dutch hoe easily outnumber the ones inadvertently beheaded by a swan neck hoe.

A garden without herbs is truly a garden without spice. Even the cheapest, meanest, most parsimonious meal can be lifted to gourmet tastes with the addition of home-grown herbs. Try some of the ones that don't package well, such as lovage, parsley, rosemary, lemon thyme, tansy. When you have your own sage plants you'll never want the dry, powdery, tasteless stuff in jars again.

Our herb collection is culinary only. If you're interested in medicinal or recreational the list obviously enlarges. The cats do go a bit funny on early spring catmint.

A fine lawn is a splendid thing, but it is expensive in time and money. It needs feeding and weeding and careful mowing and watering. A good, serviceable lawn can be much cheaper and less work. Moss can be controlled to some extent by letting the grass grow longer, and if daisies cost £5 a dozen we would pay a fortune to grow these charming little flowers in our lawns.

Time, as well as money, is to be spent wisely. Grass clippings left on the lawn feed the lawn, save your time and your money as well because you don't need lawn food. Grass clippings laboriously collected in a grass box or raked up and put onto the compost heap are a waste of time, as they will quite likely become yucky in the heap anyway. Frequently mown, the clippings will hardly show – otherwise you will find that there are lines of clippings. These can be lightly raked around or quietly ignored while you resolve to do the job sooner next time.

An old-fashioned grease band around fruit trees will collect little multilegged animals without poisoning everything else in sight at great cost.

Small plastic pots or deepish jar lids, filled with beer and sunk into the ground to their rims, are excellent traps for slugs and snails and do not endanger birds. Cover the tops with something – a slate rested on a stone or similar – so that rain doesn't wash out the beer. Empty out the dead drunkards every day or so and console yourself with the thought that they were very, very happy. Alternatively, go out at night snail-bashing.

Old window frames with most of the glass still in them make excellent cold frames.

A wooden pallet is just right for forming the base of the compost heap, allowing air to enter from the bottom of the heap. A compost heap works exactly the same as a fire.

To make the surroundings for your compost heap, there is nothing better than four wooden pallets, and you can wire them together with coat hangers.

Salt makes a cheap and effective weed-killer for use on patios. Just make up a strong solution and pour on the unwanted weeds. Try to do this during a dry period, so that the salt has time to act before it is diluted by rain. Remember that salt doesn't differentiate between weeds and your treasured plants.

You can make all kinds of gardening tools for yourself – an old piece of angle iron can easily be made into a 'gadunger' for plunging into the ground beside a deep-rooted piece of unwanted plant life.

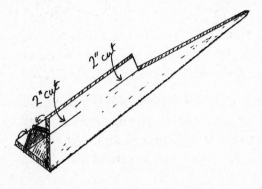

Before paying for manure from a stable or farmyard, ask around. Many stables have difficulty in getting rid of the stuff, and they will be grateful if you will take it away.

Fruit trees, if you have the land, are a good investment. They need little work and well-chosen trees will give more fruit than you can use. Here is where self-sufficiency is better than anything you can buy in the shops, because you can choose fruit trees for the best flavour, rather than weight of fruit, and most fruit loses some of its flavour between picking and selling.

There is a use for stinging nettle!! With gloves, pick a bucketful, pour water over it, cover tightly and let steep for several days – nettle tea, really. Strain out the guck, which smells godawful, dilute the juice and it is a phenomenal pick-you-up for plants.

Most garden machinery is bought by people who need it so that they can get through their gardening chores quickly, leaving them time to go down to the squash club to get the exercise they would have got if they had not used the garden machinery.

A rotavator is a mechanical device for chopping up weeds and distributing the pieces evenly around the garden in freshly-turned soil where they will prosper.

Power mowers may need servicing from time to time by a professional. Most of us wait until our mower does not start in the Spring before we send it in to be repaired, and the laws of supply and demand mean that the price of repairs at that time are at the maximum, and you have to wait for the work to be done. The same job, done in the Autumn, will be cheaper, and you are in no hurry to get the machine back.

Nut shells can be used for mulch.

Laying a hawthorn hedge is easy. Cut the height of the stems to bridge any gaps in the hedge, and then saw or chop as near to the base of the stem as possible. The thinnest strip of bark will keep the hedge alive. Always lay a hedge so that the tops of the stems point up hill, and in toward the field. Any lengths of stem cut off can be used as stakes to strengthen weak points. Forget about the twiddly bits at the top of the laid hedge. These look pretty, but are unnecessary. Wimps use gloves for this work.

If pests are eating your flowers or vegetables, heave on more manure. This will strengthen the plant and help it fight off the pest, and even if that fails, there will still be enough of the plant for you and for the pest.

Some people say there is a 'debate' between fertilisers and manure. There isn't, unless you're a complete organic gardener. Fertilisers feed the plants, but you also need the organic material to 'feed' the soil.

Manure can be applied any time, except at the same time as lime – they cancel each other out. Even carrots benefit from manure – you may get a few forked carrots, but you'll get more and better carrots.

If you are making a vegetable garden in a lawn or old pasture, and we have done this quite a few times, cut and remove any long grass, and then use a spade to cut through the turf to a full spit deep and turn it into the bottom of the hole. This will clear most of the weeds and the turf makes an excellent fertiliser.

Another way of clearing land to prepare it for planting is to cover it with a sheet of black plastic. Weigh the plastic down with stones and leave over winter. This will not kill the seeds, but it will get rid of the grass and weeds.

Leaves, even the toughest like chestnut leaves, will rot down to make compost. Corral the leaves in chicken wire to make a heap four feet or more in height. It may take two years, but you will end up with a fibrous material that will do for peat.

A garden incinerator will not only turn twigs that are too large to compost into ash phosphates, but it also lets you burn persistent weeds, such as dandelions and bindweed, that will lurk in a compost heap.

If you have to smoke, then grow your own tobacco. Tobacco grows quite well in the English climate, and the industry was only suppressed in the eighteenth century in order to protect the growers in our American colonies.

When you do have a little sunshine on your seedlings, newspaper makes a good sunshade.

For protection from the sun in the garden, wear a hat or bonnet – you can make them from old clothes.

In a dry year, some plants, such as courgettes, need watering every day. Plant the seed in a pocket of compost, then as it grows, make a little dam around the plant to keep the water where it's needed. Keep the dam repaired.

A good hedge around the garden will give extra protection from the wind and extend the Summer – never mind that the plants like this – *you* sit out and enjoy it!

Many fruit bushes will grow from cuttings taken in the Autumn.

Fruit netting pays off.

If you have gluts – plums, eggs, vegs – put them out for sale, or trade with neighbours.

Newspapers can be added to the compost heap, but you should shred them first. They are the last things to rot down, so you don't want a high percentage in the heap.

People who want manure want a few bags, while people who sell manure want to sell by the lorry-load. To keep everyone happy, get together with other gardeners and buy in bulk, each taking what they need. Once having tried the system, you will see that the same principle of cooperative bulk buying can be extended to other things. Cases of baked beans? Sacks of flour? Cases of wine?

If you are putting wooden posts into the ground, even if they will be set in concrete, their life will be extended by soaking that part of the post in used car oil.

And used car oil is just as good as new oil for using on garden tools – and bicycles – and that old wheelbarrow.

Growing your own vegetables and fruits is about as good as it gets! You don't have to be a 'good-lifer', or even live in the country; tomatoes do better on a patio than out in the ground, herbs can be on a windowsill. This, too, you can do quietly, easily, artistically, and be healthier for it!

# 7

## Getting Around on Wheels

'Steam coming out of the radiator, or elsewhere, indicated that the water was boiling, and a radiator that slowly became incandescent showed that it had finished doing so.'

W.D.H. MCCULLOUGH AND 'FOUGASSE'

Cars are so much better made than they were twenty years ago that no one need be worried about buying a car today that is a few years old. New cars depreciate fastest in their early years, and it is said that a new car loses 25% of its value when it is driven out of the showroom, because it has become second hand. It makes sense for us to take advantage of the vanity of the rest of the world, and buy our cars when they are a few years old, but still have a lot of trouble-free miles ahead of them.

Four-wheel drive vehicles are expensive to buy and they are hard on fuel. Very few people need a four-wheel drive vehicle, since very few of us have farms and estates to drive on, and the last thing Britain needs is herds of motorised nerds churning up the countryside. If you have one, stick to the roads.

In a rapidly industrialising world it is inevitable that the demand for fuel to drive this growth is going to push the finite resource, oil, to higher prices. It makes sense to buy fuel-efficient cars, and that way you can enjoy motoring at minimum expense.

Cars, like all machinery, lose value with age. This is called depreciation, and it is a real pain. One way around this is to buy a car that is going to increase in value, instead of getting cheaper – that is, buy a classic car. One of the best investments we ever made was to buy an old E-type Jaguar when nobody wanted the miserable rust-buckets. It does cost to keep a classic car in running order, but they do hold their value, and even increase, and they are fun to drive. However, fuel economy is not their strong selling point, so maybe they make a better second car. The difficulty, if you want to make money on an old car, is to know which heaps of today are going to be the classics of tomorrow.

Manufacturing cars today is a hard life, with factory output exceeding demand. Car manufacturers cut their new car prices to the bone to induce us to buy their product, but they have to make a living. They make up for the low initial price by putting a huge mark-up on the spare parts. Some repair parts have to come from the company that made the car, but most can be bought at a substantial saving from car-parts shops.

Second-hand car dealers are the lineal descendants of the old horse trader. If you buy from an individual who has advertised his car in the paper, there is a chance that he is honest.

The value of an item, including cars, is what someone will pay. Have a look at one of the buyers guide books to get an idea of the price of the car you have in mind, but you do not have to offer that much. Why not put a wad of cash in your pocket, and put in a low offer? Cash is wonderfully persuasive. Try to keep a straight face.

Second-hand cars loaded with extras are loaded with things that can go wrong.

Work out whether you need a second – or third – car, or is it just that you want one? How many times in the last year have you been truly stuck for want of a second car? Could you have rented a car, or taken a bus or a taxi? Which would be the cheaper alternative, the fare or rental, or the cost of owning and running a second car?

## More miles for your money

Petrol consumption increases sharply with speed, so slower speeds may not save your life, but it will save your pocket.

Fast acceleration takes energy, and this energy has to come from the fuel. Slow, steady acceleration is much more economical.

Heavy breaking turns the momentum of your vehicle into heat, that the brake disks then dissipate to the air. Then, when you accelerate, you use more fuel.

The above three tips may take the glamour out of driving, but they really do save money.

There is precious little evidence that one brand of petrol is better than another, so buy on price. Hunt around for the supplier with the lowest price, and try to make sure you do not have to fill up on a motorway.

80% of the price of a litre of petrol is tax.

Modern cars may be rather boring, but they are much more efficient in their use of fuel than older cars. For sheer economy it is hard to beat a small, modern car.

Large, heavy cars use more fuel than small, light ones, because it takes more energy to pull a heavy car up a hill. On the other hand, heavy cars are likely to be safer in an accident than a light one. You pays your money and you takes your choice.

High-performance cars driven hard need high-performance oils. For the rest of us the cheap oil is just as good. It is much more important for the protection of your engine to change the oil filter regularly, than it is to use an expensive oil. I know one man who did not change the oil in his car for 120,000 miles, just topping up the oil as needed. He said his oil looked like oil, smelt like oil and felt like oil, and, until someone proved otherwise, it was oil. He has a point.

Keep a little book in the car, and write down what checks and maintenance you have done, giving the date and the mileage.

This will help you remember things that should be done, and to avoid doing jobs more often than needed.

## Tyre sense

Do you know what the numbers and letters on the sides of tyres mean? Are you paying too much because you don't know?

Tyre companies go to great lengths to persuade us that their tyre is the product of advanced engineering, and, no doubt, at high speeds and under severe braking conditions, these differences are significant, but they are not going to make much difference to people who drive their cars for economy anyway. We, as customers, have to remember that companies that advertise heavily have to recoup the cost of advertising from us, so part of the cost of an expensive tyre is the cost of telling us how good it is. Shop around for the cheapest, British-made tyre, and remember to haggle.

Having bought your tyre, it will last longer if it is always at the right pressure (look in the car handbook to find that), and if the wheels are properly aligned. Wheel alignment is one of those adjustments that take a bit of special equipment, and is probably best done at a garage.

Tyre pressure, either too much or too little, shortens the life of the tyre and gives a poor driving performance. Word of this economy seems to have got around, for it is now difficult to find an air pump at a garage that does not have a queue waiting. The temptation is to drive away, vowing to check the pressure the next time you fill up. Why not get a good, sturdy, foot pump with a built-in pressure gauge, and make sure your tyres are kept at the right pressure?

It is a waste to throw away a tyre that is worn, but still legal. That worn tyre can go in the boot as the spare, and then it is only used in emergencies, and is then put back in the boot when the damaged tyre is repaired or replaced.

———————

Cars, from the day they are made, all want to return to a heap of rust, and one day they will. The secret of good maintenance is to postpone that day, making it useful to you longer. The better a car is maintained, especially its bodywork, the higher will be its second-hand price. With this in mind, we can now stand back and decide what repairs and maintenance are worth it, and what is not justified.

Unless your car is under warranty, and any repairs are going to be free from the dealer where you bought the car, it is nearly always cheaper to use an independent garage for repairs. You could find a 'home tune' mechanic who will come to your house and who can do most of the routine maintenance on most cars – and they are exceedingly reasonable in price.

Bottled soda water on a paper towel is good for getting the grime off the inside of the windscreen.

Garages are much too useful a space to be taken up by cars, and a wet car parked in a garage will stay wet, especially underneath where rots start. Either leave the car outside, where the wind will blow it dry, or keep it parked under a carport, open at all sides.

If your chosen transport is a bit of an old, rusty, banger, you may find that the lights don't come on all the time, but the problem seems to go away in wet weather. The probable cause is that the electrical earth is trying to ground on a piece of rusty steel. Rust is a poor conductor, but, when it is wet, the water helps it work. The cure is to change the earth to a solid piece of steel, free from rust and paint.

Unless an oil leak is really bad, it is going to be cheaper to top up with oil a little more frequently than it is to spend money tracing and repairing the leak. Oil that is being burnt in the engine and appears as blue smoke in the exhaust is a different matter; that has to be repaired, since it indicates serious engine wear.

Older cars get reluctant to start, especially in cold and wet weather, so a pair of jump leads kept in the boot is a good investment. Provided you have the jump leads, some kind motorist will pull up beside you and help you on your way. You will also be able to help someone else who needs a start.

In an emergency, the foil used in a pack of cigarettes can be screwed up and used in place of a fuse in a car. But this will not solve the cause of the blown fuse.

Tights and stockings can make emergency fan belts for a car to get to a garage and a proper replacement. If the tights or stockings were off a girlfriend, try to replace both these and the fan belt before taking the girlfriend home, as it could lead to a misunderstanding.

Before throwing away a leaking car radiator and replacing it with a new one, take the leaky one down to a radiator repair shop. They will strip out the damaged fins and the radiator will be as good as new for about half the cost of a replacement.

A leaking radiator far from a garage is a problem. If you try to drive to the garage, the engine may overheat and be ruined, while if you take the radiator off, you cannot drive the car at all. A solution to this problem can be to put half a cup of porridge oats in the radiator. This will form a sticky, glutinous mass that will block a small hole until a proper repair can be done.

Anti-freeze not only stops your engine from freezing up in cold weather, but it also stops corrosion in the engine block all year round.

Buy anti-freeze in the summer. As the temperature goes down, the price of anti-freeze goes up!

Batteries now come sealed-for-life, so they need no servicing. The most common reason for having a flat battery is that we have left the lights on overnight, so it is worth having a battery charger that can recharge the battery and get the car going again, without having to call out a garage.

## Bodywork

If the mechanical parts of a car go wrong, they can be replaced by buying new parts. If the bodywork rusts, then the repairs will be done by hand, and that can be expensive. Good body-work in a second-hand car is more important than good mechanical parts.

Rust never gets any better on its own, and one day your beloved car will return to a heap of rust. The sooner you act to stop rust, the cheaper it will be. If your car is showing signs of rust in the sills and other hard-to-get-at spots, try pumping Waxoyl, available from car parts shops, into the bodywork.

Although your garage has probably been turned over to a work space and a place to keep bicycles, it is a lot easier and nicer to work on a car in a covered area, rather than outside, especially in winter.

You don't need expensive chrome cleaners for your car – a little vinegar on a cloth, rub the chrome, and then give it a good rinse to get rid of the acid vinegar, followed by a polish with … newspaper.

Rainwater washes cars.

———

As in every other aspect of life, planning ahead saves money. How many journeys did you make in the car last week that could have been combined, if only you had thought about it? Those little trips to get the newspaper and pick up more milk are the ones that give you the worst mileage and cause the most wear on the engine.

A roof rack will let you carry home that chest of drawers you got at a sale, without having to pay a haulier. Since roof racks are cheap, this makes a good investment. Do not leave a roof rack on your car when it is not in use, because the extra air resistance cuts your mileage.

Towing brackets give you the flexibility to move heavy loads with your own car. When buying a new car the salesman will usually ask you if you would like one fitted, and the temptation is to agree. Since you are spending thousands on the new car, a few hundreds seem insignificant, but the same towing bracket can be bought for half the price from a motor shop, and they are easy to fit. Towing brackets also protect your car from backing into walls, and from over-friendly cars behind you.

## Getting around

If you are travelling abroad, do your own comparison-shopping between travel agents and airlines. There are some wonderful bargains, if you can adjust the time and duration of your journey to fit the special deals being offered.

If you live in the provinces and visit London, you can save time, money and temper by parking your car on the outskirts of the city, and then take tube, bus or taxi. You avoid the Congestion Charge, too.

If you regularly travel by bus or by tube, get to know your zone fares – it may be that you can get off public transport a few stops early and walk the last short distance, saving yourself the extra cost of travelling into a new zone.

If you fly quite often, then the airlines get to know you, and you are more likely than the average, nail-biting, terror-stricken passenger clinging to the edge of the seat to be upgraded to first class when the crate gets full. Most frequent fliers are flying on company business, so it is the big companies, not real human beings, who are saving money, but life is like that.

If only one person is travelling, say, into London, then it is usually cheaper to go by train. If two or more members of a family are travelling together it is much cheaper to go by car (unless, of course, you get a speeding ticket/parking ticket/ the car gets stolen, etc.).

See the paragraph above to explain the growing popularity of car pools, where only one car does the commute, and everyone shares the cost. Makes a lot of sense.

Both airlines and trains have weird and wonderful pricing structures. The only thing you can do is study train times and ticket prices, and do your best to travel at times when tickets are reasonable. Haunt the wretched station master's office, or, if they have some little corner marked 'customer service', do not take this too seriously, but go and make them earn their day's salary.

When travelling on company business, stay at the best hotels and send in enormous expense claims. This will enhance your status in the company. When travelling in Britain, or on the Continent, for that matter, and you are paying for your own accommodation, save money by staying at bed and breakfasts. You never know what you will find, so they are always interesting, and that is more than can be said for most hotels. Breakfasts tend to be vast, and seem to consist of trans fats with little bits of bacon and egg floating in it. Wonderful.

———

Donkeys are wonderful beasts of burden – 1) they are beasts and 2) they are a burden. Sweet, lovable, cute, almost a member of the family, but if you think they are going to put up with having plastic bag panniers hung on them, and they will carry your shopping home, think again.

Some animals will willingly trail a cart, a wagon, or even a sledge behind them, in which sit their happy owners plus their goods and chattels. Some animals does not include donkeys.

Much of the planet travels only by bicycle. Some countries are better organised for cycles (Holland is great!) but after taking your cycle proficiency test, you really ought to use cycles as much as possible. Just remember that you don't really own the road, and motorists aren't going to be looking out for you, especially if you weave in and out of traffic, or occasionally tag a ride on the back of a lorry by hanging on to a rear corner.

Bicycles are good for you and for the environment, so buy the best bike you can, but leave the bike gear on the shelves. The best part about biking is that you can do it in your ordinary clothes.

If you are serious about getting fit, saving the Planet, and saving money, there is no better way to do it than walking. In today's congested cities, it is often faster, too.

Britain has the world's best network of public footpaths, quite unknown to unfortunate people across the Channel. Healthy and interesting exercise is within reach of everyone, and at no cost. Your rights on a footpath are the same as those on a public road, but please shut gates and follow the Countryside Code.

A great yachtsman once said that a boat was 'a hole in the water into which you pour money'.

# 8

# Appliances – Buying, Using and Repairing

What the big print giveth ...

the small print taketh away

**Keep a file for all the instructions for your appliances and similar household purchases.** Staple the purchase receipt to the instruction booklet.

If all else fails, READ THE INSTRUCTIONS.

Learn how to diagnose faults when an appliance fails to work by first looking through the instruction booklet. There would probably be a a call-out charge when the only problem might be, for example, that the cooker is on timed programme and therefore won't come on manually. I have had a wonderful washing machine repairman who kindly pointed out that my machine wouldn't pump out because it was perishing cold outdoors and the drains were frozen, and there was no call-out charge, but gems such as he are few and far between, believe me.

Consider the extended-service warranties available for most domestic appliances, but CAREFULLY – they can be very expensive. The ones that probably are worthwhile are for the machines using water and with lots of moving parts, which are washing machines and dishwashers. Cookers, fridges and freezers are pretty reliable old things, as are sewing machines.

The most versatile, useful, satisfying, labour-and-money-saving appliance is a sewing machine. From darning socks to making wedding dresses. No other appliance will save so much and give such rewards. There are often free lessons when buying new and these build confidence for those who do not know how to sew. A good basic electronic machine with free arm, zig-zag and possibly programmed buttonholes is all that is required. Few other appliances last 20 or 30 years.

Keep the sewing machine clean, oil it *as required*, USE THE TENSION control, don't use blunt or bent needles. Give it the care it deserves!

ALL appliances work more efficiently if they are kept clean. Nicer to be near, too.

It is more efficient to boil water in an electric kettle than on the cooker in a saucepan … boil only as much as needed! Less waste, less wattage.

If there is leftover boiled water from the kettle, when just cool it freezes faster, because it has less air in it, and makes clearer ice cubes.

Keep kettles descaled – vinegar works, unless your instruction book forbids it. Empty the kettle completely after use and there won't be any water in it to make the scale in the first place.

Empty: vacuum cleaner bags, washing machine filters, dryer lint traps, dishwasher strainers – and kettles. Do it often.

Many people find that night-time cheap rate electricity works well for them, but remember that you have to have the life-style to make it worthwhile – everything you use during the day is charged at a higher rate than the normal domestic rate. Invest in a programme-timer so that your appliances such as the washing machine actually work during those cheaper hours … if you (and your neighbours) can sleep through all the noise and you are happy in your own mind that you won't wake up to a plumber's nightmare.

Before calling in the repairman for a noisy appliance, check that it is on a level surface. Even electric typewriters and sewing machines make a funny noise if they're not level.

Check the seals on appliances – if a piece of paper slips through a closed door, the seal is not a good fit and money oozes out, whether the appliance heats or cools.

## Cut your cooking costs

Make sure that bottoms of saucepans are flat to heat evenly and efficiently. If they aren't flat, fram the daylights out of them with a wooden mallet until they are. They can also be ground or scraped down with metalworking tools.

When baking is finished, having turned off the oven early, of course, open the oven door to let the heat out which is also better for the oven inside, as then the moisture doesn't condense. Be sure that small children aren't hovering too close.

Pressure cookers do make wonderful stews in a fraction of the time taken on a cooker, but we did watch in amazement once as our supper streamed upwards to the ceiling.

Not so much an appliance, but an expensive pot: get the best and largest steamer you can afford, especially if you grow your own vegetables. In the early part of the summer there are often small amounts of five or six different vegetables, and steaming is the very best way of cooking vegetables anytime, the flavours do not mingle in the baskets, and far less time, water and watts needed.

Microwaves are fast! Wonderful for thawing frozen foods. Does some things better than others – get a good microwave cook-book. Much lower wattage (around 650) than cooker ovens (2000 and more), but it's too easy to slip into boring ready-made meals if they are over-used. Now there are microwaves combined with a small conventional oven.

Water can be heated to boiling. Full stop. Once it has boiled, TURN DOWN THE HEAT. It doesn't get any hotter than that, and the heat will be wasted as well as the water evaporating.

Put oven shelves in position BEFORE switching on the oven.

Oven cleaners, quite harsh chemicals, aren't needed if the oven is kept clean all the time. Make it a habit to wipe it out each time while it's still slightly warm – even if it's just with news-paper, it helps. Clean is more economical.

Ovens can be wiped with a bicarbonate of soda and water mix-ture to help keep them clean.

Aga ovens don't need cleaning, but a new Aga is an awesome price.

———

Breadmakers have come down to what is laughably called popular prices. Having made bread by hand since I was a teenager and loved doing it, there is a lot to be said FOR a bread machine, especially for smaller families. We use it constantly.

Our food processor is over 20 years old, still wonderful, but the oft-replaced bowls are rubbish 'built-in obsolescence'. I was never afraid of flying until the booklet mentioned they were made of the same material as aircraft windows.

A dishwasher is a dishwasher, not a garbage disposal unit. Scrape the food off the dishes before loading – you would for the washing-up bowl – so that the machine runs efficiently and lasts longer.

Beware the environmentally-friendly words 'economy cycle, extra £30' when buying a dishwasher – not even the salesman would say that the way it worked was that it completely left out the drying cycle!!!

Don't buy more technology than you need in appliances – most people use only two or three cycles on most machines.

## Laundry economies

A small Y-shaped device, available from DIY or plumbers' shops, to close off the hot tap to the washing machine will allow a cold-fill only. This usually costs less than using hot water from the central water heater, and it gets the clothes cleaner.

Washing machines seem to prefer one load a day rather than several loads in one day. I don't know why.

It will take less detergent if clothes are soaked before washing, and most machines now have a delay switch.

Use a water softener such as Calgon if you live in a hard-water area, it keeps scale crud away, you can use lots less detergent, and the machine will probably last longer with less trouble.

Washable wool and a wool cycle – unbeatable!

If clothes are too damp after a low-speed spin, re-spin them, it's the same as using a higher speed but less wrinkles.

Drying clothes takes expensive heat if it is done in the dryer. Using the clothes-line is the best way, for the sun and wind are free. In our unreliable climate it is useful to have an indoor place to dry things.

Use the airing cupboard to dry laundry. Store linens some-where else. Use any constant heat for the best purpose.

Work out wattage: dryer 2500. Iron 1200. Now work out how long it takes to iron five shirts, let's say an hour (don't you just hate maths?). It will take 1200 watts. Five shirts in the tumble dryer, though, will take about 20 minutes, or one-third of an hour, and 2500 divided by 3 = 833.333333333333 (aren't cal-culators great?) – 833 watts wins. Plus all that time saved!

Iron only as a last resort. Iron only what shows. Let the iron do the work with its heat, it isn't a steam roller that needs your muscle power.

If thick 'luxurious' towels pong from being too wet too long, put them through the washing machine using Dettol or simi-lar instead of detergent. When the wash is finished, run them straight back through, normal wash with detergent and a fabric softener or a little white vinegar as a rinse. Works on anything.

## Cooling control

Appliances that cool (fridge or freezer) shouldn't be placed adjacent to ones that heat (cooker, boiler).

A freezer is a money-saver! Especially if there is home-grown produce, but also for pick-your-own and special offers from butcher and greengrocer. Save transport costs and time by shopping less often.

A full freezer is more economical to run than an empty or half-empty one. No problem for those who grow their own, but for those who don't, plastic containers of water fill all the empty space in the freezer.

Know what you want to get out of the refrigerator or freezer before you open the door, so you don't stand gawping at the inside while you let the cold air (which cost you money) swirl outside, neutralising the warm air (which probably cost you money), and the warm air whoosh inside …

To make defrosting a freezer a little bit easier, put several layers of newspaper in the bottom when you've emptied it, and you can empty out newspaper, frost and water all in one go.

## Heating control

If you have central heating, watch the bill like a hawk!

Turn down the thermostat, make sure you can control the radiators. Individual controls for each radiator are one of the best investments you can make for economy. This can't be repeated too often.

Turn down the temperature on the water heater, even if by only one or two degrees.

Use fewer hours on timed water heating – experiment until you can ACTUALLY notice a difference or everybody moans.

Keep out major draughts! Some ventilation is needed, but not a howling gale.

Double layers work at windows, too. Curtain linings make a tremendous difference, particularly if they're hung on separate hooks from the curtains themselves, trapping warm air in the space.

Curtains hung over draughty doorways keep the heat in and the cold out.

If radiators are under windows, use short curtains above them so the heat is inside the room. A couple of long curtain drops can be put at either side.

Foil can be put behind radiators to help reflect the heat, and a shelf over radiators both deflects the heat into the room and helps prevent dark heat marks on the wall. But do put up the foil before fitting the radiators – it's difficult afterwards.

A hot water bottle is cheaper than an electric blanket. Have you ever had a hot salt pillow? (This is superb, by the way, for ear-ache.)

For fireplaces: Stretch your fuel by making newspaper logs. A logroller can be used, but the papers can just be rolled good and tight and wedged into a box to help keep the shape. If there's plenty of free string, tie the rolls. It still seems illogical, but they don't unroll in the fire – they look even more loglike as they burn.

Everybody has their favourite way of making firelighters from newspapers – roll them, scrunch them, fold them, twist them.

Take advantage of any free wood. Ask the farmer about the fallen tree before you haul it off. Another source of free wood is from woodworking shops, they will be grateful if you take away their waste wood, which can be a problem for them, a godsend for you.

If you use coal, do make up briquettes with the coal dust and a tiny amount of cement and water.

Eliminate draughts by covering unused fireplaces. Just leave a ventilation area so that air can circulate in the chimney and room. Stuff balls of newspaper in draughty, unused chimneys – not in ones you're using, though!

Multifuel heaters are truly that. We watched in fascination as an acquaintance threw an old Wellington boot into the flames!

Compare prices of fuels! There's a wider choice in towns, but country gardens grow a lot of wood.

## If it's broke, can you fix it?

The secret of repairing washing machines, irons, anything you are unfamiliar with, is to note very carefully how you took it apart. Perhaps you have a digital camera as you go along and can refer to it frequently.

Household appliances are all big investments and they can all go wrong. Cookers, vacuum cleaners, washing machines, dish-washers, clothes dryers, the list goes on, so it is worth thinking about how they can be repaired and their lives can be extended.

The first thing to note is that they are all electrical, so unplug from the mains supply before taking machines apart. You will need some type of mains tester so that you can check whether current is reaching a part of the appliance. You will need screwdrivers – slot head and Phillips – to take the appliance apart.

Since all the machines run on electricity, it is not surprising that most faults are electrical. Wires break, bayonet connections get shaken loose, and most common of all, a bare connection has shorted out against the steel frame of the appliance. Taking care, follow the current from power in to each part of the appliance until you can identify the fault. Oven fans, for instance, can be taken out and replaced, dryer drive belts wear out and will need renewing, sewing machine foot controls wear out, but all of these repairs are within the abilities of most people. Domestic appliances are not rocket science.

Libraries have books about repairing appliances, so off you go.

————

TV – Turn it OFF. Really OFF, not on standby. Even the electricity companies recommend this.

Low energy light bulbs are supposed to be extremely economical, but our own experience has been that they blow even faster than conventional ones, at about seven times the cost. They also become dimmer over time.

On the minus side, low energy light bulbs contain mercury and should not be disposed of except as hazardous waste.

These bulbs make most sense where lights are left on for long periods, such as hallways, bathrooms and porches, but bearing in mind the comments above, they are probably not the miracle answer they seemed to be, though there would likely be a small saving over a year.

Use the vacuum cleaner dusting brush! Dust cloths shift dust around, vacuuming removes it quickly if not so quietly.

Some pets enjoy being vacuumed, and those that don't can eventually be scraped off the ceiling.

Cats make ridiculously expensive mouse traps, but their cost looks more reasonable if they are classified under Entertainment.

# 9

# Good Food – The Foundation of Good Health

Better is a dinner of herbs where love is, than a stalled ox and hatred therewith.

PROVERBS 15:17

Make living better for less a pleasure. You will save money and time by planning your menus, so why not plan a month at a time, rather than just a week? Make that a trip-round-the-world month. Have Italian-style meals one week, Australian another, Russian the third and American the fourth. Go to the library and you will find super cookery books – pick and choose the dishes you can cook with home-grown, IN-SEASON, ingredients: keep to warm-climate countries during the summer and cooler countries for winter's cabbage, turnips and sprouts. By planning ahead, you will know on the 4th of the month whether you will need more rice before the 29th of the month. If you won't … don't buy any.

Supermarkets have made 'seasonal' foods available just about year-round, but take the time to learn when foods are

abundant or scarce, where they can be bought at local outlets such as markets, small greengrocers', a local farmer. They will be 'seasonal', fresh, economical and not suffering from jet lag.

Foods, too, have 'fashions'. Last year's miracle-cure food is this year's poison.

Take pride in cooking things yourself! Don't apologise for homemade goodies, you know what went into them … and what didn't.

Make your own junk food snacks, they are delicious: potato skin crisps – when you're doing roast potatoes and have scrubbed them clean, put the peels onto a baking tray with a *tiny* amount of oil, salt if wanted, stir to lightly coat with the oil and tuck into the oven for about 10 minutes. A whole potato can be done this way as well, slicing it quite thinly, much healthier than bought crisps.

Homemade biscuits and cakes don't need preservatives because they don't last that long.

No mushrooms? Use carrot slices instead – crunchy, cheap, especially if you grew them yourself.

Sliced or grated carrot and a bit of garlic are also a reasonable substitute for onion!

Remember that the cheaper cuts of meat are just as nutritious as the expensive ones. You are NOT depriving yourself or your family of nourishment by choosing cheaper cuts.

Don't be afraid to be adventurous – if chicken is on special this week and you had planned a dish of pork, the chicken can probably be substituted.

Evaporated milk can be diluted with a bit of extra water for use in cooking, and is a good substitute for 'cream' as it comes out of the tin.

Use less flour for coating meat by measuring a small amount into a paper or plastic bag, then add the meat and shake.

A beer bottle is a superb meat tenderiser. Hit the meat directly, not at an angle, with the small open end.

Use food tins to steam foods – especially if you have small amounts to cook. You can even throw them away after you've used them once.

Anything from a bottle of ginger ale to drained fruit syrup or leftover desserts can be frozen to make ice lollies or 'ice creams'.

If cornflakes have become limp, they can be crisped in an oven (while something else is baking). Or use them as a casserole topping.

You can re-use coffee grounds by baking them for half an hour or so in a moderate oven (you know I'm going to say it) WHILE SOMETHING ELSE IS BAKING.

Make your own beer.

Our secret recipe for hamburgers – people at our barbecues always ask for it: find a local farm or a real butcher. One pound (450 – 500g) of mince makes 4 burgers. That's it. Add nothing. Salt and pepper as it grills.

Mix your own muesli, and add extra oats to bought muesli.

Buy a bag of economy frozen peas for everyday use rather than expensive petit pois. They differ little in taste, lots in cost.

Make a batch of fudge or clotted cream fudge or toffee using evaporated milk.

Add the last bit of a meat loaf to a tin of tomatoes for a pasta sauce, giving you a whole extra meal.

Just because a tin of anchovies has ten fillets in it doesn't mean you have to use all ten in the recipe calling for a tin of anchovies. Use fewer – say half – and the other half can be used a day or so later in another recipe. Keep the remaining half covered tightly in a dish, not the tin, in the fridge. Don't let them rot there.

If you are pouring all the cream from a container let ALL the cream drain out.

If you always keep a little rice and pasta in the cupboard, it won't be a disaster if you then forget to buy potatoes.

Doesn't a still, quiet little voice inside say that rice lasts longer than the 'best before' date on the packet. Read what it says: BEST before, not throw it out the day after that date.

Don't limit pickle-making to chutney. Go to the library if necessary for a cookery book, but homemade pickles should be unique every year.

Homemade water biscuits or oatcakes are special!

Line the bottom of the salad drawer in the fridge with newspaper or paper towels to help keep vegetables fresher longer.

And bread DOES keep better in the fridge, in a bag.

Reduce stale bread to crumbs. Freeze only what you will actually use in a reasonable time – feed the rest to the birds, for goodness sake!

'Convenience foods' are always more expensive than conventional, and conventional ones are more expensive than homemade or homegrown.

'Empty' sauce bottles often have enough left to dilute with water, milk or vinegar for an extra serving or more. Add to dishes being cooked.

You don't have to have greaseproof paper. Brown or white paper, brushed over with whatever oil or fat you're using, works as well now as it did for decades. And if you want the most delicious ham you've ever tasted, do it as they did in the Old South: bake it inside a heavy brown paper bag, then remove the bag, take off the skin, and score the fat in diamonds. Put a whole clove into each diamond, cover the lot with a mixture of brown sugar and American mustard, and pop back into the oven for about 20-25 minutes to glaze.

Apple peels are edible. Cooked apple peels are still edible.

When you've melted chocolate in a SMALL saucepan, don't rinse it out. Let it dry and then scrape it out for chocolate decoration.

You can stretch your coffee by adding roasted, ground soya beans, or ground roasted chicory root.

Leftover egg yolk is maddening – either plan to have scrambled egg with extra yolk straight away, or put the yolk into a small container and cover with water. Keep in the fridge, preferably only one day – otherwise it lurks.

Gravy can be made out of nothing: heat a little oil or fat in a heavy frying pan. Add flour and let it brown – not beige – brown. Add hot stock (made with a stock cube or the real stuff), a sprinkle of herbs, stir until it resembles gravy.

"For a delightful luncheon...slivers of leftover roast pheasant on thin brown bread...a wedge of pale crisp lettuce with blue cheese dressing...a succulent fresh peach, with a glass of cool, clear Sauterne..."

To keep lettuce fresh longer, rinse it still on its stalk, shake it as dry as you can and then keep it in a plastic bag in the fridge. Of course this isn't something you have to do if you've grown your own lettuces, you're usually trying to think of some way to use up several at a time.

Broccoli is edible. Broccoli leaves are edible. Broccoli stalk is edible. Broccoli flowers are edible.

Cooked lettuce is delicious. Leftover salad can be boiled and whizzed into soup, but also good is a fresh lettuce in a casserole dish with a little hot stock – cover and bake for about 20 minutes.

Whole rolled oats, lightly toasted, make a reasonable substitute for chopped nuts.

Rice is reheatable, so don't throw leftover away – just rinse it, and gently reheat in its own steam.

Rice freezes well. Reheat from frozen as above.

Bacon part-rashers/pieces/bits save time and money for using in casseroles.

If you have never made your own sausages you are missing a lot! Delicious made into links, but not half bad just as sausage patties. Varieties are almost endless, and you know what goes into them!

Why buy cooked meats such as chicken loaf or even salami when it's so easy to make your own? If you can make a meat loaf, you can do it.

A cut onion stores on a saucer, with a bowl turned upside down to cover it.

If you do a lot of baking, you may find that a real (and expensive!) vanilla bean is a bargain – fill a jar with sugar, and bury the vanilla bean in it. The sugar will be vanilla-flavoured, and you just keep refilling the jar with sugar. For years. The Roman epicure, Apicius, did this sort of thing with the herb silphium as it was eaten out of existence.

Like the vanilla bean, you can grate orange or lemon rind and add to sugar, delicious for making biscuits, but doesn't keep so long – do it about a week beforehand.

Homegrown tomatoes are SO delicious. Grow them in pots on the patio. Wrap them individually in newspaper and stack them in greengrocers' boxes in a cool, dark place, or in cupboard drawers to ripen over the autumn, and you should still have your own fresh tomatoes for Christmas dinner.

Freeze tomatoes. Wash, dry, put into bags the minute they ripen, to be thrown still frozen into stews and casseroles for fresh-tomato taste. Don't expect to slice frozen tomato for salad, though – they just won't cooperate.

Simmer leftover juice from stewed fruit for a little bit of jam that can be stored in the fridge. It will thicken a bit more as it sits there.

Good, satisfying food doesn't need expensive 'dressing up' to be appetising.

Make your own bread, and discover how it ought to taste. Handmade or machine.

Jam-making has an undeserved reputation for being tricky. It's a piece of cake, and a real illustration of living better for less. If you haven't grown your own fruit, go pick some or buy some. Wash it, weigh it, put it in a pan. Now add HALF its weight in sugar. Yes, half! Depending on how juicy the fruit is, you add a LITTLE BIT of water, but don't drown it, you only have to boil it off again. Now mash the fruit and SIMMER the lot until it's thickened – it will then look slightly transparent, i.e., it will look a bit like jam! Do not fiddle around with thermometers or pectin or skimming away any of your jam – it's all edible – or paraffin wax or anything else you have to go out and buy. Just put the stuff into clean jars. Now the small print: make small batches at a time, and store in the refrigerator. Put the rest of the fruit into the freezer to make more small batches during the year.

Not everybody on the planet has a refrigerator. It is quite possible to live to a ripe old age without ever having had one – otherwise none of us would be here now, would we? If you need to keep something cool and the fridge is bulging to its seams with food – say at Christmas time when we all try to empty the food shops – and outside is too cold, think of the wine cooler! All you need to do is surround it with cold water. In a sweltering hot climate, milk – unpasteurised, unhomogenised, unirradiated, natural milk – is kept fridge-cool by putting it into a demijohn, tying a rope around the handle and lowering it into the water well.

Somehow pastry never fits the piedish. Even if it does we feel compelled to trim the edges and fiddle around making patterns. Since the oven will be hot, either fling a little bit of jam on scraps of leftover pastry or add some grated cheese to make straws, but DON'T put that pastry into fridge or freezer thinking you'll make something later. You won't, you'll waste the pastry. Do it now, while the oven is ready.

Pasta is one of the great foods of the world. It is user-friendly, compatible with just about anything, satisfying, inexpensive, long-lasting and a real budget stretcher.

A delicious way to cook sausages – or even other meats – and keep them from shrinking: put them into a frying pan with a little water (hot or cold), COVER the pan and simmer. Now watch them carefully and let the water evaporate, and the sausages brown.

When eggs are expensive, learn to use substitutes in baking: a smaller egg will make precious little difference in a recipe.

Some egg substitutes: 1 teaspoon of vinegar equals 1 egg, as does 1 teaspoon cornflour plus a bit extra water. So does an extra half teaspoon of baking powder. Soya flour is another substitute which is most useful. Use 1 Tablespoon soya flour, 1 Tablespoon water. Custard powder can be used in the same way – it's mostly cornflour anyway.

Don't bother freezing eggs. You have to separate them, then add either sugar or salt to the yolks, you'll NEVER get a fool-proof system of marking, and the dratted little packages slither to the bottom of the freezer anyway, to join the infinitesimally small plastic blob of yellowish red greasy crevassed leftover spag bog that was to have been a midweek lunch if you could just have found it before you got frostbite.

Especially if you live in the countryside, you really ought to keep chickens for at least a year or two. You will know how a fresh egg ought to taste, you will learn that about 50 per cent of the chicks are male and therefore exceedingly delicious, and you will never, ever feel soppy about a fox again.

Food processors or liquidisers make reasonable caster sugar. For icing sugar, add a little cornflour, it's never so fine as bought icing sugar, but saves a trip to the shop in a pinch.

Make your own yogurt by starting off with a good spoonful of natural yogurt per pint of warmed milk. No need for expensive equipment, a wide-mouth vacuum flask can be used, or just let it sit on the worktop in a jar until it 'yogs' and then put it in the fridge. Add some milk powder to the warm milk for a thicker yogurt, but you're aiming for homemade, not commercial.

Honey is a super substitute for sugar – especially if you have your own beehives. Just omit 2 ounces of liquid in a recipe for each 8 ounce (225g) substitution.

When you bake a chicken, SAVE the fat. Pour it into a small container such as a ramekin, cover and store in the fridge. It lasts for weeks, and is delicious in cooking, a small spoonful is superior to stock cubes or powder.

Save bacon fat, too, as above. A small amount is all that is needed for soups that need bacon flavour.

Save every bit of fat from all meats. A mixture of fats makes perfectly good shortening and cooking fat. Save butter and olive oil for special purposes.

Learn how to render fat and clarify it. Don't let fat scraps sit around to become rancid – they're useless then. Even birds reject rancid fat. The easiest way is to put the scraps of fat into a tin and put into the oven while something else is baking at a low to moderate temperature. Pour off the melted fat as it accumulates into a suitable storage jar, keep in the fridge.

To clarify fat which has sediments in it, simply add water, bring to boiling to melt all the fat, and let it cool. Skim off the clean fat which will have risen to the top and solidified.

Vegetarians avert your eyes now. The average person needs about four ounces (100g) of meat per day, and this is enough, you don't have to eat the whole animal at one sitting. Meat is one of the most expensive elements of the food budget, but don't let vegetarians convince you that they live all that cheaply, because they often seem to spend a FORTUNE on supplements, pills, vitamins, minerals and all those things that God so thoughtfully provided in meat. (And He added meat-eating teeth in our mouth, as well.)

Rabbit is delicious. Pigeon is delicious. Anyone who lives in the countryside already knows this – the information is here for townies. It is difficult to see why one shouldn't eat rabbit and pigeon, because rabbit and pigeon will do their utmost to eat everything in one's vegetable garden.

Game is very healthy meat. Go find a good game merchant.

Keep a store of tinned and dried milk. Use them in cooking and baking, and keep the more expensive fresh milk for drinking and using in tea and coffee. You can add more water than the diluting directions suggest.

Make your own sour cream by adding a little lemon juice to single cream. Or a little vinegar. Stir in a bit of milk powder to make it thicker.

To keep from wasting things like biscuit dough, pasta dough, and pastry by re-rolling and throwing away scraps from around the circles you cut, don't cut circles – cut squares.

If biscuits have gone limp, a few minutes in the oven will revive them, preferably while something else is baking, otherwise it could be cheaper to buy more biscuits!

Any leftover meat or fish can be turned into paté with the flick of a switch on a food processor or the turn of a handle on a mincer. Add a bit of butter, a dash of cream if it's around, some imaginative flavours with herb, spice or bottle, a final slurp of alcohol if there is any.

A barbecue doesn't have to be an expensive steak or chop affair – belly pork makes a wonderful meal, with a sprig of rosemary or sage on the fire if you grow your herbs.

Eggs aren't necessary in coating batter – the lightest, crispest batter is made of just water and SELF-RAISING flour.

To serve only expensive food and wine at a dinner party is to confirm what your guests suspect: that you have no imagination. A free out-of-the-garden starter: a ramekin of puréed spinach with a strip of cooked sorrel on top. An almost-free dinner-party-quality wine: elderflower, sparkling if desired.

There is a theory that if you buy smaller plates, you will then serve up smaller meals and people won't particularly notice. We bought smaller plates, and now have messier tablecloths than before.

Have you ever eaten baked beans? Real ones? Find a recipe – or write to us and we'll send you ours.

It is quite permissible to buy Sainsbury's dry sherry and pour it into a decanter to serve to guests. It is not permissible to buy Sainsbury's and pour it into a Tio Pepe bottle to serve.

If you are budgeting, there is no reason why your pets should live high off the hog. Downgrade their food as well, they won't starve. Pets lived on leftover scraps for most of history – they will even eat porridge … eventually.

Learn to love soup, and have one meal a week which is 'scrap' soup – the tag ends of celery, carrot, sweetcorn and peas, a piece of apple or pear, even bacon rinds.

## Make your own wine and beer

Homemade wines are a cheap and efficient way of getting drunk.

Nearly all fruits and most vegetables can be fermented, but some give better results than others.

Fruit, especially fruit like apples, can often be had for free if you see the fruit dropping off the trees, and you ask for it. It would be polite to repay your kind benefactor by giving him a bottle or two.

Books on wine-making at home make a great thing of cleanliness and sterilising, but this is not necessary. Ordinary home cleanliness is sufficient.

Homemade wine can be stored in good strong plastic drinks bottles. Real corks are harder and harder to find nowadays, though it's more fun to store wine on its side in a rack.

---

If school lunches cost £1 a day, experiment to see how exotic a packed meal you can prepare for 50p.

Plastic lunch boxes for the children look good for the first week, but then the catch breaks. With a cheerful piece of cloth, some wadding or foam rubber, you can make a lunch bag that will be the envy of your child's schoolfriends.

Faddy eaters are a real pain and expense. Our rule is that children are allowed one food they can refuse, and after that, they can eat up or shut up, and no snacks. My own rule is that I will at least try any food that is eaten by men who wear trousers. If they wear sarongs or grass skirts, I will reserve judgement, but otherwise I will have a go.

During periods of watching the budget, can you put your hand on your heart and say you don't still buy CORNFLAKES? Or crisps?

Use newspaper as a substitute for paper towels when you have to mop up spills or absorb grease.

## Vinegar in cooking

You can tenderise meat by soaking in water to which a little bit of vinegar has been added. This is often used for venison and other game to make them a bit milder in taste and tender in texture.

A reasonable substitute for wine in cooking is a little bit of vinegar added to tomato puree and water.

If you have a supply of dried peas or beans which take an age to cook and are still tough, use a little bit of vinegar in the soaking water.

_____

When you've picked your hops or herbs, hang them in bags made of tights or a sleeve from an old shirt.

A 28 lb (12 kilo) bag of potatoes from the supermarket usually costs about the same as a 56 lb (25 kilo) bag from the local farm shop.

Baby food is a fine commodity, since it comes in convenient packages and takes no preparation. Just the thing for baby on a long journey. For baby's meals at home it is much cheaper, and better for the child, to use a mixer or dice the food you eat. This gets him used to your food, rather than the tastes of the commercial stuff. Go easy on the vindaloo, though.

Turkey is a festival food, but it is also cheap, so if there is a family festival coming up, serve turkey.

Soaking old dried fruits in water revives them, soaking them in sherry or brandy revives the spirits.

**10**

# Clothes that Fit the Budget and Fashion

My mother always said 'a patch is honourable, but a patch *on* a patch is a disgrace.'

If you have kept a garment for years without wearing it, you probably like the fabric but not the style – or size. Can it be re-made?

Never throw away or recycle a garment before removing the buttons, zips and useful trimmings.

Make tiny spools from spirals of card, save those last yards of thread in a pretty box and keep for repairs.

Keep matching buttons together with a loop of thread, or loosely stitch them to a piece of card, or keep in a tiny container.

Darn that pair of socks as soon as there's a hole in one of them.

Patterned fabrics show creases far less than plain ones do, so are much better for travel.

You can make everything you wear – sheer tights and out-door shoes would present a little difficulty, admittedly, but other than that you are only limited by what you want to make.

At jumble sales, look carefully at how a garment is made – is there enough fabric in a full gathered skirt to make a shirt and trousers for a child? Look for a skirt with only one centre back or front seam. Carefully removed from the waistband, you will find a generous stretch of fabric. Cost for shirt and trousers for a three-year-old girl, including buttons as well if you're lucky: around 10p.

Put on a pair of cotton gloves before you put on a sheer pair of tights to prevent snagging.

Old-fashioned but wonderful: thermal underwear. Look for them at market stalls.

Insoles, especially thermal ones, make enough difference to your foot comfort to merit going out and buying them! You can also make them from several layers of newspapers, though these tend to wrinkle – but then they cost nothing to replace.

Get to know your local shoe repair man – but ask how much a repair is going to be! They vary around the country, and a simple re-heel job can cost more than the shoes did.

When you have bought a new pair of tights, you can make them last longer by a little attention BEFORE you ever wear them: it is said that they will last longer if you freeze them overnight; one doesn't know why, but since it doesn't cost anything it's worth doing.

Another process said to prolong the life of your tights is to wash them before you wear them, preferably by hand. Use soap, not detergent. Plunge the tights into lukewarm water, getting them completely wet. Rub the soap onto your hands, not directly onto the tights. Get a nice sudsy lather, and gently wash with a squishing, not rubbing, motion, rinse thoroughly, blot with a towel, and let dry naturally.

Thick tights – unless they hurt in tight shoes – are truly 'warmer tights'.

Wash tights or other delicate clothes in a bag … made from old tights.

Hang lavender, etc., in tight-bags in the wardrobe.

Wear the panty part of tights (the legs of which you've cut away for other uses) as 'thermals' over ordinary underwear.

Stiletto heels are an ugly fashion, the cause of sprained ankles to the wearer, and damage to all types of flooring. The use of stilettos should be restricted to Sicilian bandits.

Never throw away an old T-shirt! Not only dust cloths and cleaning cloths, but shirts for smaller people, strips and bits sewn together to make enormous, long snuggly nightgowns, strips cut off the sleeves to make headbands. Blessings to the person who invented T-shirts!

Mend holes in your pockets the minute you see them – money falls out.

Protect good clothes in the wardrobe by putting an old shirt over them.

Never throw away a jacket just because the lining has given up the ghost. Carefully unpick the lining, press it and use as the pattern for cutting a new one.

If you're making something in corduroy, remember that while the colour is darker if the nap runs UP, the article of clothing will last longer if the nap runs DOWN.

If you can crochet, you can make superb braid to match your jackets, etc., by using embroidery threads. And you can embroider with sewing thread.

Socks can be darned on a sewing machine if there is a free-arm on it, and by using polyester thread the darn is probably a lot stronger than the sock surrounding it.

Search out small sewing shops which may stock industrial-quality and strength threads. It is the aim of clothing manufacturers to ensure that the home seamstress can never find good quality makings, but seek and ye shall often win.

If you don't already have one, go and buy a fine, steel, crochet hook. Every time you see a loose thread on any garment, use the hook to yoick it to the inside.

Reinforce, reinforce, reinforce. Wherever clothes are likely to wear, spend five minutes when you first get them putting in just a few extra stitches whether by machine or hand.

Children's clothes are rarely worn out by one child – they are outgrown first. Therefore, they should be sturdy, but cheap and cheerful. Never spend big money on small people's clothes, unless you have numerous small people to whom they will be handed down.

Have some kind of handy reference for stain removal. Most stains will wash out, but usually quick action is the vital ingredient. Don't spend more on stain removal than the article is worth. Admit defeat and add it to the ragbag or dressing-up box.

BUT FIRST have a go at doing some deft embroidery over or around the stain.

Brushing your clothes is still one of the best things you can do for them, it keeps the dust and dirt from working their way into the fibres, and is less damaging to the clothes than laundering them.

In the case of MUD on clothes, ignore the ubiquitous advice to deal with a stain the minute it happens, because if you start scrubbing mud around you *will have* a stain, but left alone to dry completely, it can be brushed or vacuumed up – whether on clothes, carpet or upholstery. Make sure the brush you use is dry or you're back to Square One.

If you have dribbled food onto your clothes, do not hang them back up in the closet!! Get it out, because that's what attracts moths, they like food.

Colour-coordinated wardrobe? Buy one basic colour and stick to that? When hell freezes over. Why be boring? One of the joys of living better for less is having lots of clothes for very little money, and if you want an orange outfit, have one. It doesn't HAVE to match anything else in your wardrobe.

Elegance doesn't have to cost pounds. Like beauty and integrity, it comes from within. You really can dress well from charity shops and jumble sales. Stand up straight, hold your head up, and walk tall.

You can actually save money by having a suit made by a tailor. How? Have TWO or even more pairs of trousers made which will extend the life of the suit several times over. How many times have you reluctantly discarded a perfectly good jacket because the trousers were worn out at the seat?

Buy clothes or fabrics that do not require dry cleaning. Use the dry cleaners only for very best, tailor-made suits and high-day-and-holiday wear.

Search around near you to find mill shops, factory outlets and shoe discount stores – and this gets harder all the time as manufacturing moves abroad. Prices in these shops, though, are far below those in the high street, and there should be little or no difference in quality.

Well-kept clothes last a lot longer than neglected ones, and look better as well.

For keeping sweaters looking good, there is a wonderful little comb-like gadget called D.Fuzz.It. which costs a few pence and can usually be found in markets or household shops. These were tucked into Christmas stockings one year and have been treasured ever since!

Hang up good clothes the minute you take them off – but not straight into the wardrobe, first check and remove spots, and let clothes air in the room first.

If you don't have enough wardrobe space for your clothes, you can make your own multiple-level coat hangers by clipping one hanger over another's neck. Then your clothes won't be crushed so badly.

If you are serious about saving money, and say that you can't sew, then learn how to sew!

When you make your own clothes, buy the best quality fabric that you can afford – it will still work out a lot cheaper than buying readymade. You will find good bargains in mill shops – name-brand fabrics at a fraction of their high street price.

Even less expensive than buying new fabric is buying good fabric already made up – at jumble sale or charity shop. By

buying large sizes or full-gathered skirts you will have a generous amount of fabric to play with, and even if you make a mistake it won't have been an expensive one.

Pattern pieces can be placed much closer together than shown on cutting-out diagrams, often saving a quarter yard (23 cm).

Multi-size patterns are very useful if you, like most of the other people in this world, are not a standard size. You can choose the bits that fit YOU.

A very easy way of dealing with collars is to not have one.

## Make your own patterns

You can start with an old favourite garment, take it apart, iron it, and there's your pattern.

You don't have to take a garment apart to make a good pattern. Lay the article of clothing on a large piece of paper – wallpaper or brown paper, my own favourite is silicon baking paper in large rolls – and pin it down along the seam lines as far as you can go without distorting the garment, tracing around the shapes, unpinning as necessary. Sometimes you'll have to make an educated guess as to where a line should go, but when you've taken the garment away, you'll be able to 'join up the dots' and then ADD ON A SEAM ALLOWANCE. If it looks a bit wonky, don't panic, just straighten up the lines a bit – you're clever enough to know not to cut warped seams.

Sewing without a pattern is scary only the first time you do it.

Large sheets of newspaper are perfectly adequate for making your own clothes patterns, but plain paper is much easier for early efforts.

Large envelopes are just right for saving the patterns you've made yourself – a sketch on the outside, title on the top corner. Sketch of layout, notes on construction.

————

The '70s and '80s made blue jean cut-offs popular for everyone, but some of us have done it for years, first making pedal pushers, then when their knees wore through you got Bermuda shorts and finally short shorts.

If there's a place on your tights that always wears, find the chair/table/shoe which is snagging them. Fix it.

By all means choose a basic colour for your expensive clothes, but do let yourself relax in cheap and cheerful colours by spending less money on casual clothes.

To help keep moths from invading your sweaters, make sure the garments are quite clean, then gently steam-iron, make sure they're absolutely dry, and wrap them in newspaper for their summer holiday. If they are very pale in colour, wrap them first in tissue paper or even an old shirt.

Before putting knitted clothes, or even sweatshirt materials, through the washing machine, turn them inside out to prevent 'pilling'. Some are worse than others, but this simple method really works.

Clothes and shoes are expensive, so take good care of them. Keep them clean, mended, hang them up to 'rest' after you've worn them, and try to let them rest for a whole day before you wear them again. They will last longer and look better. If you possibly can, alternate your shoes, as well.

To keep your shoes in shape, or to slightly stretch a snug pair, stuff newspaper in them while they're still warm after wearing. And if you are cursed with smelly feet, sprinkle some bicarbonate of soda in with them for a truly refreshing change.

Our French friend has an excellent method of keeping shoes fresh – she fills old socks with lavender and tucks them into shoes: they fit perfectly, make use of old socks, and as she points out, she'd have to buy bicarbonate of soda but the lavender is free from the garden!

You don't ever have to buy shoe polish. If you have leather shoes, you can polish them with the beeswax-turpentine polish you've made for your furniture – superb for walking boots! Patent leather can be cleaned with vaseline or the inside of a banana skin.

Repair shoes the minute they need it and remember, if high heels get scraped they can often be camouflaged with a felt tip pen.

## Is there anything you can't do with vinegar?

Summer fruit and grass stains can often be removed by soaking in vinegar before laundering.

When altering a hemline, dab vinegar on the crease and then iron dry. No telltale line left!

You can even remove chewing gum from your clothes – just use vinegar!

To treat perspiration stains on clothes, soak in a little vinegar water before laundering.

––––––––

Most bought interfacings are too stiff, and rarely keep their new appearance; domestic irons just aren't hot enough to truly weld the 'iron-on' ones. Much better interfacing comes from old shirts, or just scraps of cotton/polyester curtain lining fabric, or washed muslin.

You can use a much-loved but perhaps out-of-date shirt or large blouse as a jacket lining.

Superb nightshirts can be made by removing the collar (if there is one) from your husband's old school shirts. De-cuff it, and

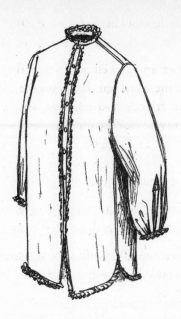

stitch together the sleeve opening. Stitch pre-gathered eyelet edging (broderie Anglaise) all around the neck, cuffs and bottom edges.

Men's trousers have an undeserved reputation for being difficult to make. The best pattern, though, is the pair that has fallen apart from having been worn constantly – take them apart, and make educated guesses about where the seam line would have fallen when they were first made.

You can usually rescue a felted sweater. Wash in that wonderful wool cycle, minimum temperature, or wash by hand, and use a fabric rinse with either method. Shake out really hard, stretch like mad, and hang on a big plastic hanger to dry, away from heat. Keep on stretching as it dries, every time you walk past it stretch the daylights out of it. Do not be tempted to nail it onto a board as in blocking, it's the stretching AS IT DRIES that works.

Children's clothes are so well made that they are outgrown before they become worn out. It is a simple economy to swap clothes between friends and relatives, so that the children always have plenty of clothes and the clothes are put to good use. I am told that the Queen passed clothes down from one child to the next, and if it is good enough for Her Majesty, it is good enough for the rest of us.

Nobody, neither man, woman nor child, needs astronomically-priced trainers. Even trainers don't need them.

Don't dress up at home. Scruffs are comfortable. Keep your good clothes for outside occasions, so they look their best. The same goes for shoes.

'Economical' does not mean 'inelegant'.

# Looking Good – Make-up and Grooming

> Though we travel the world over to find the beautiful we must
> carry it with us or we find it not.
>
> EMERSON

Toothpaste, we have always said, is not one of life's necessities –
though this sometimes brings gasps of amazement from
younger people who thought it was around on the Ark.
Toothpaste is bought not because it cleans the teeth but
because it makes the mouth feel good and fresh (I am not
making this up, it's marketing knowledge). If you brush your
teeth long enough, they'll get clean, and tooth sticks or dental
floss work. Brushing stimulates the gums, which is a good
thing. Some of the simplest and best breath fresheners are parsley, caraway seed, coriander seeds, or cloves. Sage leaves are
also used for cleaning teeth, dried ones can be crumbled and
added to salt and/or soda for a tooth powder.

Make your own facial: Use a TINY amount of olive oil to
cleanse your face well. Spread the white of an egg (as is or

lightly beaten, as you wish) over face and neck. Leave on 15-30 minutes, then rinse off with warm water.

Make your own bath additives: oatmeal or herbs in a sachet made of old tights, milk straight from the powdered milk box, lemon from the fruit or the bottle.

Bath oil is simple but not so attractive as bought, it separates, and they're all slippery in the tub. Mix half-and-half cheapest vegetable oil and washing-up liquid. A drop of scent if available. Shake furiously before each use.

Save all small attractive jars for homemade cosmetics.

Nail polish lasts longer if kept in the fridge.

Even used teabags can be used in beauty rituals. Some women put them as a compress on their eyes to relieve tiredness, others use them as hair colouring. Somehow they seem more useful to houseplants and compost heaps.

If you have percolated coffee, the grounds should either be put onto the compost heap or straight onto garden or pot plants, but you can use them first as a hand scrub, especially after gardening.

## Some things our mothers always told us

These things cost absolutely nothing, but contribute to looking good in public:

Learn to BE STILL – don't fidget.

Don't touch your hair or your face. It's terribly bad for your face, as well.

Sit up straight.

Hold your head up and your lips shut.

---

Oatmeal really, truly, honestly does make your hands wonderfully soft and smooth. Trust me. Oatmeal soap is a reasonable substitute, but if you could bear squishing your leftover porridge through your hands every day – preferably several times a day – you would be pleased with the result!

Dry lemon and orange peels, pulverize in processor, coffee grinder or mortar and pestle. Keep dry. Add some oil to make a face mask. Add a little peel to bicarbonate of soda or soda-and-salt for brushing your teeth.

Lemon juice makes a super hair setting lotion. Use it neat. Hair is soft and silky after you brush it.

Lemon juice, rosemary or beer all make good hair rinses.

Make your own lemony shampoo: shave about a bar of soap into a saucepan, cover with water, heat gently until soap melts. If it's thicker than you want, add more water. Add lemon juice.

There is precious little difference between expensive scents and inexpensive ones except the amount of advertising done by the expensive ones.

Baby lotion is a good make-up remover, baby cream and baby oil are quite suitable for grown-up faces, and you don't have to own a baby to buy baby products.

If you use cotton wool balls, do make your own from rolls of cotton wool sold at chemists'.

Don't let your hands become chapped and rough – DRY THEM completely before going outside in cold weather. Learn to wear gloves. You won't need lotions and potions to get soft and smooth hands.

Take care of your hands by avoiding expensive cleaners! They are ALL harsh – just check how many have 'rinse hands after use' on the labels. Neither vinegar nor bicarbonate of soda are tough on your skin – quite the contrary.

If you push back your cuticles with your towel as you dry after every bath, you can do without cuticle remover.

Simply massaging your nails helps keep them healthy and shiny.

## Hair care cuts

One really good haircut a year can be more economical than going to the hairdressers' every few weeks for mediocre cuts. This applies to women only, sorry chaps – back to the barber, or talk someone near and dear into learning how to cut your hair.

Grow your hair long. Or learn to cut it yourself. Forget curls unless God gave them to you.

In warm weather, let your hair dry naturally. Cold weather is unkind to hair – wear a hat.

Another way of cutting the cost of hair care is to be a model, but I think you have to accept whatever hairdo is being created or practiced. Some hairdressers also have certain days on which prices are lower than others.

———

You will always get gifts at Christmas, so let people know if you actually like perfume oil or luxurious bath products. It gives them great pleasure to give them to you, and it gives you great pleasure to know that you didn't buy them.

Make your own bath lotions and potions – don't forgo the relaxing pleasure of fun bath products.

A very small container of perfume oil will last for AGES – you only need a few drops in bath water or homemade cosmetics.

You can use half the kitchen cupboard to naturally cleanse the make-up from your face: vegetable oil, mayonnaise, yogurt, lemon juice, egg (yolk, white, both beaten, plain, stirred), smashed-up cucumber, tomato ...

Make lovely little lipstick pots – use tiny little jars from other cosmetic products or gift jam jars – by gently melting down odds and ends of lipstick and combining with a little vaseline for your 'designer lip gloss'.

There is a wonderful colour consultant: your mirror. Look deep into its eyes and if you like the colour you are wearing, it suits you. Generally, your friends-and-relations will remark on flattering – or ghastly – colours, and they are usually right.

If there are colours you love but that really don't look good on you, have your cake and eat it, too, by using them in just little accents and accessories.

Keep scent bottles securely closed, preferably in their boxes, in a dark place, not sitting prettily on your dressing table exposed to sunlight.

Add a few drops of your favourite scent to unperfumed talcum powder and shake well.

Loo paper isn't all THAT different from tissues.

You can use lipstick as blusher if you use just a tiny bit.

It's easy to do your own expensive-salon type hot oil treatment for your hair. Cost: not a lot. Any cooking oil will do it, from cheapest own-brand vegetable oil to gourmet olive. All you have to do is heat the oil to a COMFORTABLE temperature, apply to your scalp and comb through all of your hair. For even more luxury, wrap your head with a hot towel and leave until you're bored. Shampoo and rinse.

When you do the egg white facial, you can use the yolk for a hair treatment. Separate the egg, and do your hair first with the egg yolk – trust me, it feels yucky, but it does leave your hair feeling silky – you can wrap it in a hot towel, or just leave it on for half an hour or while you're doing the facial. Finally, rinse off the white from your face, then the yolk from your hair – the latter takes some rinsing to get it all out. Your hair and skin feel wonderful – one egg and a bit of hot water!

## The ever versatile vinegar

If you have sensitive skin, you may well find that hair conditioners are an irritant. A money-saving substitute for these –

which is much more natural and closer to your skin's pH balance – is vinegar. You only need an ounce or so, diluted if you wish in a mug of water.

You can use vinegar as a deodorant, just wipe on with a cloth. Like bicarbonate of soda, though, it won't stop you perspiring.

To soothe sunburn, you can use vinegar.

Relieve itching skin – anywhere – with vinegar. No need for expensive creams and lotions.

To keep sponges and loofahs fresh, give them an overnight soak in water with a little vinegar, then rinse and let dry.

For an inexpensive and easy mouthwash, use one tablespoon of vinegar in a glass of water. Sprinkle in a spice such as cloves if you like.

Soak smelly socks in 1 part vinegar, 5 parts water before laundering.

If you have athlete's foot, soak your socks in vinegar-water before laundering, and apply neat vinegar to your feet.

————————

If you use shampoo on your hair every day, then your scalp gets hysterical from all the removal of natural oils, and it itches. This makes you use more shampoo. Wonderful for shampoo manufacturers, bad news for scalps.

Herb shampoos, rinses, bath additives, all are yours for almost free if you have a small herb garden, and you enjoy the beauty of the garden as well, for herbs are most attractive little plants. Easiest of all are simple infusions of herbs with boiling water – tea, really. Try camomile for blonde hair, rosemary for brunette, lavender for the bath. You can even use pine needles as a substitute for that expensive one.

Aloe vera is a miracle plant. Keep one in the kitchen for breaking off a leaf and squeezing the juice onto burns. It is unsurpassed for insect bites, taking the itch away so you don't claw at them.

A most pleasant hand cream is made by mixing rosewater and glycerine, about half-and-half. A drop of perfume oil can be added, but hardly a necessity.

The most wonderful lip salve EVER: gently melt a couple of tablespoons of beeswax. Stir in a teaspoon or so of honey, then beat in two to four tablespoons of oil – any kind – two spoons giving a firm product, four a softer one. Pour into tiny jars or pots. This is also the most superb hand cream you will ever come across, and it is suitable for men, women and children.

You can do your own – ouch – waxing of legs with hot beeswax. (This rates right up there with contact lenses: both are possible, but sound too painful even to contemplate – this is definitely for offspring.)

If you do make many of your own cosmetics, you might like to know that borax and beeswax in combination are used as emulsifier (to keep mixtures from separating). I've never bothered, because it only adds to the cost, and I make them for using, not selling.

Another kitchen ingredient to keep in the medicine cupboard – honey is antiseptic, spread a little over shaving nicks.

One of the more luxurious baths: add a little honey.

If bicarbonate of soda doesn't appeal as a toothpaste, try a little bit of honey – Hippocrates suggested using it on a ball of wool.

Use honey as a face mask – either on its own, or in many, many combinations.

You can save great amounts of money by not buying nourishing creams, night creams, day creams, vitamin creams and above all wrinkle creams. Never resent growing old, so many are denied the privilege.

Scientists have been unable to discover any difference between expensive lipsticks and the cheap ones.

'Costly thy habit as thy purse can buy.' As true today as when Polonius first uttered the advice to his son, Laertes. Not for nothing does Shakespeare survive.